FAITH'S
FREEDOM

FAITH'S FREEDOM

A Classic Spirituality for Contemporary Christians

LUKE T. JOHNSON

FORTRESS PRESS ▪ MINNEAPOLIS

FAITH'S FREEDOM
A Classic Spirituality for Contemporary Christians

Library of Congress Cataloging-in-Publication Data

Johnson, Luke Timothy.
    Faith's freedom : a classic spirituality for contemporary
Christians / Luke Timothy Johnson.
        p.   cm.
    Includes bibliographical references.
    ISBN 0-8006-2428-9
    1. Spirituality.   2. Spiritual life.   3. Christian life—1960–
I. Title.
    BV4501.2.J558   1990
    248.4—dc20   90-32839
                                                              CIP

The paper used in this publication meets the minimum requirements of American National Standard for Information Sciences—Permanence of Paper for Printed Library Materials, ANSI Z329.48-1984.

Manufactured in the U.S.A.   AF 1-2428

94   93   92   91   90   1   2   3   4   5   6   7   8   9   10

In Memory of Friends:
Pius Lartigue O.S.B.
John Hollar
and
In Gratitude to Guides:
David Melançon O.S.B.
Andrew Becnel O.S.B.

AD PATREM!

Contents

Preface

The author of any book on spirituality appears, by the simple fact of writing such a book, to be making certain claims: to know what God is up to in the world, or to have reached whatever state of perfection the book describes. At least that is what I always assumed when I used to make a habit of reading such books; more than that, I believed those implicit claims.

Just in case you who have picked up this book should make the same assumption, I assure you that I make no such claims. I can barely figure out my own mind, much less God's. And as for sanctity, ask my family or my students.

What I say about God and perfection I say from the earth up, not from heaven down. I think of theology as a catch-up ballgame. God is always ahead of our thinking, and much of what we call theology is guesswork. My guesses may be wilder than most. I am an expert in some aspects of this topic: I know all about idolatry, fear, compulsion and sin from the inside; that's my metier. But I have also been touched by the Other and by gift, and I am trying to figure out what to do about that, and what to think about that.

Anyone who wants to do this kind of thinking called theology must be careful not to claim too much. I am aware of the limitations of this book; it does not have a cosmic scope; it is loaded with the sort of perceptions one would expect from a middle-aged white American male (more than slightly overweight). The data I work with come from the tradition in which I was raised and which I still affirm with more or less enthusiasm, my own story and that of the people I have lived with, and the many stories I have been privileged to hear over the past twenty-five years of careful listening.

Although this is highly personal thinking, I have tried to make it rigorous. There is an argument running from beginning to end. It will not appeal to everyone. Some will not like the premises. Others will dislike my characterization of other spiritualities. Still others will observe that I have borrowed from other thinkers more or less accurately without giving them credit.

I am unapologetic about all these deficiencies. I recognize that my premises derive from a highly traditional understanding of Christianity. I know that my way of describing gnostic and liberation models of spirituality does not correspond to any specific author but is a caricature based on popular renditions of those perspectives. I acknowledge that any good ideas here come from better thinkers before me, but in fact they have now become my ideas and are all mixed up with ideas from other places, and sorting it all out is pointless. All I ask of the reader is the willingness to think with the argument from one end of the book to the other, and then decide whether it makes sense.

Pieces of the argument were worked out over a long period of time. To the patient listeners who endured the earlier versions, I extend my thanks. They include the Sisters of Mercy at the 1971 House of Prayer in Biloxi, Mississippi; the folks at Villanova University who sat through a lecture titled "Worldly Spirituality" in 1982, and those at St. Mark's Cathedral in Seattle, Washington, who heard a three-lecture version in 1985. Thanks as well to the Congregations and Clergy Conferences in Connecticut, New York, Maryland, Louisiana, Illinois, Wisconsin, Ohio, and Indiana who shared with me their hospitality and their responses to my ideas.

The most important forum for developing this book was the course I offered at Yale Divinity School called "Christian Existence as Life in the Spirit." Nancy Heslin, Flo Lidell and David Lamarre-Vincent worked with me on the pilot version in 1980. A year later, some sixty students worked through the same material, and I learned a great deal about the value of the ideas from their personal responses and in their journals, the reading of which counts as one of the most edifying experiences of my life. Among those in recent years who have been willing conversation partners and readers I gladly thank Julie Galambush, Gayle Williams, Bill Shepherd, Mary Jo Weaver, Sandra Pate, Terri Covington, Laura Jackson, Jeff Fry, Jan

Fuller, Bryan Whitfield, Carla Valentine, and especially Barry Jay Seltser who has co-authored this book in ways he may not fully appreciate.

My deepest gratitude as always is to Joy, who by remaining always other has remained always grace in my life, the most powerful experience of God's love that I have been given.

Introduction

Christian faith is something to be lived before it is something to be thought about. As something people live, faith adapts itself constantly to changing circumstances, otherwise it would not be faith but stubbornness. As something to be thought about, faith must also translate itself within ever-changing circumstances, which include changing symbols and ideas. This is the task of theology.

Spirituality is faith seeking depth and maturity. It is the quest for sanctity, the individual person's commitment to authentic Christian existence. Spirituality must also adapt itself to a changing world both in action and in thought.

We may still read with pleasure and even profit Thomas à Kempis's *Imitation of Christ*, the *Cloud of Unknowing*, or even Thomas Merton's *Seeds of Contemplation*. But if we are reading them faithfully, we must constantly translate them from the categories and perceptions of another world to those of the one we inhabit today, from sets of assumptions that make no sense to us to others that do. The gap between the world of Thomas Merton and our own, indeed, is surely greater than that between Thomas à Kempis and Thomas Merton!

Christian spirituality needs an intellectual recasting that takes seriously the life of ordinary people in a world shaped by modernity rather than the monastery. But it needs a recasting that is faithful to the fundamental experiences and convictions that define Christian existence, not a translation that is actually a betrayal to a contemporary ethos.

The need exists despite the large numbers of books on spirituality that appear in bookstores, for three qualities of those books are glaringly apparent. The first is that they have little grounding in specifically Christian theology. The second is that, apart from discourse about prayer, they rarely touch on the problems of real life. Above all, most current spiritualities take for granted what cannot be taken for granted: that the basic framework of Christian faith is understood and accepted by readers.

The goal of this book is to make the sort of connections between theology and life that specialists and popularists alike seem to assume already known. My experience and observation suggests just the opposite: very few people really know how belief in one God and prayer fit together, how the gift of the Spirit and suffering inform each other. It is not enough to be encouraged to prayer and silence. I must have as well some intellectual grasp of how silence and the obedience of faith work together, and how faith and love are articulations of the same basic response to reality.

A Fragmented Christian Language

Making these connections is not easy, but it never has been. The problems are not entirely new: Theology has often been divorced from the life of the church, and piety has frequently been uninformed by theology. But the problem of recasting spirituality for contemporary Christians is particularly difficult for three reasons.

One reason is the sociological displacement of serious theology from the church to the university, together with the ever-increasing specialization of academic fields. Even within theology, subdisciplines spiral crazily away from the center. A symptom is the proliferation of adjectival theology. The traditional subdivisions of theology into doctrinal and systematic and pastoral were bad enough. A systematic theologian could thrive in complete ignorance of a biblical theologian's work. The recent multiplication of adjectives is more ominous, however, revealing a tendency to define theology itself by terms that function grammatically as adjectives but in reality define agendas: liberation theology, process theology, political theology, and so forth. These adjectives can point to a legitimate subtopic of discourse about God. Too often they indicate exclusive claims about how one can legitimately talk about God.

Second, the separation between theology and life is exacerbated by the breakdown of traditional catechesis within churches. In Roman Catholicism, the entire post-Vatican II generation has grown up ignorant of the basic creed and culture that earlier generations had imbibed from birth. The erosion of tradition in Protestant denominations is less spectacular but equally destructive. Ask any seminary professor: schools of ministry draw as students adult converts who are ignorant of the Apostles' Creed and the Lord's Prayer. Seminaries often try to lead such students from the catechumenate to ministry in three years.

The fragmentation of Christian symbolism is even more obvious among laypeople, which points to the third reason why any translation of spirituality today is difficult: language and meaning in general are overwhelmingly fragmented in the culture of mass media, dominated by ersatz psychology and sociology, the jargon of glitz and glamour, thus leaving the language and meaning of Christian faith in tatters. Christianity is becoming linguistically dysfunctional! The words of faith simply do not signify much even to those who continue to use them. The language of theology is certainly too arcane for life. The language of daily life seems impervious to theological interpretation. Ask a Christian what grace or sin means. The confusion in the answer will be matched by the respondent's difficulty in applying such terms to the complexity of everyday circumstances.

Words only make sense within a coherent linguistic system. If theological terms do not connect with each other, then they do not make sense. If they do not connect to our lives, they are not useful to our lives. If I can point to nothing in my life I can term grace, then the symbol has no meaning in my life. And if the word grace has no referent either in theology or in life, then it is literally nonsensical.

It matters tremendously what words we use to describe and interpret our experiences. If my only fluent language is that of psychology, then psychological categories shape my perception and experience of life. I may claim my faith language is important. But if I cannot apply it to anything real, then it is less important than the language I can use. I may be able to speak of a nervous breakdown but I will not see or speak of the same experience as a conversion. I will think in terms of sickness but not in terms of sin.

Making Connections.   This book tries to reinvigorate some basic Christian words by connecting them to the language in which they make sense, and by connecting them to our everyday experience of life. I want to make faith as identifiable as potatoes, and sin as specific as salad. To do this, we must pay considerable attention to the basic truths we confess as Christians. In this sense the present book truly is a primer. It deals with what is most basic, because what is most basic is also what is most important.

Consequently, this is also in most ways a profoundly conservative book. I call what I am describing "a classic spirituality." A word of clarification may prove helpful. I do not mean to claim that I am writing a spiritual classic that will endure! Nor am I taking a classic spirituality (such as that of the Desert Fathers) and making it available to contemporaries. Rather, I am trying to make a coherent case for a spirituality that is classically Christian. By this, I mean three things. First, a spirituality that is based squarely on the creed (specifically the Nicene Creed) which was shared by all Christians up to the time of pure biblicists. Second, a spirituality based on the canon of Scripture. Third, a spirituality that is at once specific and elastic, that has room for diversity but also genuine integrity.

I begin with the Christian creed. I try to enliven some of its articles, not because they are irrelevant, but because they are most relevant. I try to show how the statements of the creed join together in something more than an abstract declaration concerning what God might be out there. Properly understood, they provide a magnificent vision of what God's life is meant to be in here.

Models of Spirituality

A way into our topic is provided by asking the simple question, "What is Christian perfection?" If the word perfection raises the specter of perfectionism, we can remind ourselves that in the New Testament the Greek word for perfect is *teleios*, which simply means mature. Our question, then, concerns the way Christian life develops from its beginning to its full realization. Another way of asking our question is therefore, "What does the mature Christian look like?" A still more traditional phrasing would be, "What is a Christian saint?"

Some will instinctively answer the question in terms of personal self-control and fulfillment. The saint is peaceful: untormented and unconfused. The saint is apathetic, experiencing neither desire nor anger. The saint has achieved a higher level of awareness and enlightenment, a sense of unity with the divine. This image has an impressive pedigree in the great Eastern religions. In Christianity, it appeared in the second century movement called Gnosticism. Gnosticism completely reinterpreted Christianity in terms of indi-- vidual transformation. Although suppressed, it continued in mod- ified form to offer one of the most compelling visions of Christian perfection, through underground movements such as Catharism and more directly through the practice of monks and mystics. Throughout this book, I refer to it as the gnostic model of spirituality.

The word model is used deliberately. Ideas like perfection or maturity make sense within an overall understanding of an organic process. If we talk about human perfection or maturity as a goal still to be reached, we imply that something is lacking that needs to be supplied, something green that desires growth. A spirituality is the process of moving from the beginning state to the finished. But spirituality is itself a secondary concept. It depends on a more fundamental idea, salvation. A spirituality operates within a system of salvation.

Any system of salvation, in turn, involves a way of understanding the world and humanity, their respective origins and destinies. The study of religion has developed a technical vocabulary for these matters, which it is helpful to learn. Not only can we thereby say things faster, but we can use the terms later in the book and not have to redefine them. A system of salvation is called a *soteriology*. What I want to show is that every soteriology implies as well a cosmology, an anthropology, and an eschatology. These terms re- quire some explanation as well.

To say that one is saved, after all, raises at once certain basic questions: saved from what? by whom? for what end? and in what way? If I answer, my "self" has been saved, I have given only a partial answer. What is this "self"? Is it the same as the empirical ego that interacts with the world, or an "essential self" hidden from sight? Is it separate from the body, or does it include the body? Still another set of questions would be raised if we answered that what is saved is the people, or the world. Each of those answers would also require definition, and lead to the overall soteriology we im- plicitly are invoking.

A *cosmology*, then, is an understanding of the world: where does it come from? Is it essentially bad, or good? Is *part* of it bad or good? If so, which part? Does any part of it have a future? Is that future tied up with my own or with ours? An *anthropology* is an understanding of humanity. What is the human person, and how composed? What is the meaning of terms like soul and body? Is one better than the other? Does one have a future and the other not? Is the soul part of God, and the body part of the world? And if God is good and the world bad, does that mean my spirit is good and my body bad? For that matter, is the subject of salvation only "I" or is it "We"? Are persons defined in isolation or as part of society? Is it the person or a people that is to be saved? An *eschatology* is a vision of the future, the final resolution of things. Is the world an illusion within which eternal souls pass through stages of transformation on the way to their place of origin? Is the world real and good and itself headed for transformation? Will *we* or only *I* be around at the end?

A model of spirituality operates within some such system of salvation. Its answer concerning perfection implies an answer to all these other questions. The answers are not, of course, always made explicit. Sometimes they must be inferred from the style of spirituality itself. If, for example, I define prayer in terms of unity with the divine, I suggest at once something about the capacity of humans to attain such unity, and also something about the nature of the divine. There are only a handful of models of spirituality. The gnostic model is one.

The Gnostic Model.   The gnostic image of sanctity is compelling. It takes seriously personal transformation and growth. It has a coherent understanding of God and of the human person; it makes sense of prayer. It appreciates the power of appetites and passions. The image also has severe limitations. It works best for Christians who can remove themselves from activity and live in contemplative communities. The model finds little positive appreciation of body, emotions, society or church. It makes no direct connection between the authentic self and the neighbor. It has difficulty thinking what to do with "the world" beyond fleeing it.

Models of spirituality can appear in secular form. The gnostic model surfaces today in various "self-awareness" therapies and programs. Instead of prayer, there is imaging and meditation; instead of *apatheia*, cool; in place of inspiration, being clear; rather than fasting, diet; instead of vigils, jogging. But salvation is still of the self; the means is self-control. The grand mythology of religious soteriology has disappeared, with its account of the world's origin and destiny, with its dramaturgy of good and evil in battle for the soul. All that remains are the sad mechanisms of self-protection and preservation.

Even in its original religious form, however, the gnostic model has only an uneasy connection to the Christian creed and finds little example in the Jesus of the Gospels. For a spirituality that regards salvation as the freeing of the soul from the body, it is difficult to know what to do with the confession, "we believe in the resurrection of the dead and the life of the world to come." For an understanding of perfection as self-control it is hard to find an exemplar in the Jesus who wept for a friend's death and over a city's fate; who flashed in anger at his enemies, and who "with loud cries and tears" (Heb. 5:7) sweat blood before his own death (Luke 22:24).

The Liberation Model. For many Christians, another understanding of perfection has replaced the gnostic model. I call it the liberation model. In this vision, sanctity is demonstrated not by the mystic but by the activist. The mature Christian is not one whose soul communes with God, but one who expresses solidarity with suffering humanity. The human problem is less entanglement in the body with its passions, than enslavement by oppressive social systems. Salvation is not the liberation of the individual person's soul from the suffering caused by fear and desire, but the deliverance of whole populations from their condition of social marginality.

In the liberation model, a Christian reaches maturity in passionate engagement with social change. The living God is a God in process of becoming. Those who do justice on the earth are the agents of God's self-realization. The vision of humanity is less individual than collective. People in conditions of social oppression have not yet reached their full potential as persons, their inheritance. Only when they have realized equality of rights with their oppressors are they "saved."

The cosmology of the liberation model is the exact opposite of the gnostic. The physical world is not evil but good; indeed, it represents all the good that humans have. To think of spirit as a realm distinguishable from the physical or even superior to it is to be alienated from one's own true condition. Cultivating the spirit is therefore counter-revolutionary, a self indulgence that holds back the salvation of the people who are hungry, dispossessed, enslaved, raped, and scorned. As for eschatology, the liberation vision of the future also excludes as alienating the hope for a heaven or hell that would rectify earthly injustice. The "world to come" is understood as one of transformed social structures within which our children, if not ourselves, can achieve their full humanity in conditions of equality, freedom, and solidarity.

The liberation model is powerful and internally coherent. Whether it is essentially Christian in the sense that it derives from distinctly Christian perceptions of reality is not certain. At times, it appears to use Christian rhetoric as clothing for a vision of reality derived from something other than the gospel. Its great popularity today— especially among clerics and intellectuals far removed from conditions of acute social deprivation—owes much to its capacity to mobilize moral passion. In particular, it energizes a sense of compassion for the neighbor lacking entirely in the gnostic model.

When the only alternative forms of spirituality amount to little more than self-indulgent exercises in growth and realization, it is not surprising that Christians who can see the suffering around them should seize on this model of Christian perfection. They may at times grow uncomfortable at the thought that by the terms of this model Che Guevara has as much claim to be considered a saint as Mother Teresa. They may hesitate over the fact that the blessings of God in this vision sound a great deal more like the blessings of Deuteronomy for long life, prosperity, and possession of the land, than the beatitudes of Jesus. They may worry over the possibility that the legitimation of hostility toward oppressors or even of violence to overturn structures of violence ill accords with a Messiah who preached love and forbade retribution.

Such Christians may hesitate at the transvaluation (amounting at times to elimination) of such fundamental Christian convictions as the resurrection of the dead. They may pause over the realization that out of the whole New Testament they can find positive significance in only a handful of verses. Paul they can scarcely use at all, and they look less to the Jesus described by the Gospels than the Jesus reconstructed on the lines of their social agenda. They may mourn the loss of introspection and prayer. They may grieve that the only spirituality allowed by this model is that of merging one's freedom into the spirit of revolution. They may long for a God who does not depend on their marching that day in picket line. But they are in the end willing to trade intellectual coherence and Christian tradition for a vision that can engage their commitment to the world. And if those are the options, who can blame them?

I have briefly sketched the gnostic and liberation models of Christian life in order to show that the question "What is the shape of Christian maturity?" is capable of being answered in quite distinct ways. In the course of this book, I will return to each when discussing specific topics. The point is not to controvert the models and certainly not to condemn those who live within them, but only to locate more precisely the understanding of Christian life I am describing. I begin that description by listing some of its essential components.

Basic Convictions

The Christian understanding of the spiritual life does not begin either with the cultivation of some higher aspect of humanity called "the spirit," or an immersion in the spirit of history. It means rather "life in the Spirit of God." Our most fundamental conviction is that we are not alone in the world, either for purposes of escape from it or for purposes of transforming it according to our own image. Instead, we are creatures essentially aligned with a power never directly seen but always implicitly present: God who is Spirit. God is not simply a name or a logical deduction. God is power, the most important actor in the drama whose smaller parts we find ourselves playing.

The path to Christian perfection (maturity, sanctity) begins and ends in encounter with this Other who is always ahead of us, always active. In the first part of this book, I will delineate more carefully what I think we can appropriately say or not say about God. It is essential to state from the beginning, however, that Christian spirituality is not a process of internal grooming but a response of human freedom to a higher and more elusive freedom.

Among other important corollaries to this conviction, one can be stated immediately. Perfection in Christian life is found in the *process* of response itself, not in some completed product. The process ends (from our perspective) in death, never before. God may not be in process but we certainly are. This is good news.

Since Christian life is essentially a path of response to a living God who powerfully if invisibly intrudes in the structures of human life, then spirituality also is intrinsically physical. No Christian spirituality can pretend to be adequate that stops with the cultivation of the soul. We implicitly engage God when we engage the world. Our bodies mediate the engagement of God's freedom with ours. Our bodies extend our selves into the physical world, and are symbols of our self-disposition. More than that, our bodies are also the means by which God's freedom encounters other persons. Two chapters of this book will examine the complexities of bodily existence.

A straightforward corollary of taking the body seriously is a positive appreciation of emotions. They may be confusing, but they are essential. Their precise role needs clarification. But Christian spirituality cannot involve the suppression or denial of emotions, those that are uncomfortable or ugly any more than those that are pleasant. The emotions play a critical diagnostic function in the spiritual life: they are the truest indicators of our actual projects in the world. They help us figure out what is really going on in our lives.

If Christian spirituality involves the body, it also thereby involves society. Humans are essentially rather than optionally social. So, we have been led to believe, is God. The fact of human society is critical for the understanding of Christian life I am describing in this book. That we encounter others in the world, and not simply the Other, enables us to make sense of our life of faith in terms as real as potatoes. We live in complex sets of social structures and systems. We are born into, are imprinted by, separate from, and form new families. We join clubs and associations and churches. We belong to and participate in the structures, activities and symbols of towns and cities and states. Our self is unintelligible apart from these multiple relationships. We do not encounter God apart from them but through them.

Taking the social character of human life seriously means that our approach to spirituality must be appropriately flexible. A critical deficiency in the two models of spirituality I have sketched is that each oversimplifies the relationship of the self to the world. In the gnostic model, self-realization is thought to be possible in isolation from others. In the liberation model, perfection is found in engagement with the political action necessary to shape the large movements of history. The spiritual life for some is found in contemplating the navel, for others in scanning the headlines. Some seek meaning in biorhythms or others in revolutions. Some are transformed by meditation, others by militancy. These models swing us between the extremes of privatism and publicity. Each of them alienates us from our specific and all too bodily lives, by transporting us either into the controllable world of contemplation, or the manipulable world of political activism. Each of them misses the essential matrix for the life of faith, the human community we encounter every day.

Plan of the Book

Based on these convictions, I propose to develop an argument concerning the path toward Christian maturity. The essential framework is provided by the classic Christian creed. This Rule of Faith developed in the first place in response to perceived misinterpretations of Christian experience and conviction. It provides the historical Christian community's key to the Scripture. In the writings of the Bible—most directly and critically in the writings of the New Testament—we find the God-inspired reflections of the first Christians on their experience of God in Jesus and the implications of that experience for their life together in the world. These writings in the deepest sense authorize our own thinking about our lives. They author Christian identity in those who read them faithfully. And they authorize by their open-endedness new understandings of the same God whose Spirit enlivened and enlightened them, and who now encounters us.

Only occasionally in this book will I enter into a close reading of specific Scripture texts. One cannot do everything at once. I must ask the reader to trust that my entire vision of how these things fit together derives from those writings, both as they have challenged my life and those of others to deeper understanding. Although I usually use the RSV translation, I sometimes work directly from the Greek in order to derive a certain reading. In particular, my argument concerning Christian maturity derives from the letters of Paul, not in isolation from and certainly not in opposition to the other New Testament writings, but rather as the witness who most explicitly considered this question that now faces us: how is the pattern of the Messiah replicated by the Spirit in the lives of disciples, so that the story of Jesus is continually told in the multiple and diverse narratives of other human beings?

In the first two chapters I will develop more fully some of the ideas I have sketched in this introduction. I will consider in turn critical concepts about God and about human existence. These chapters provide the basis for a consideration of the human walk that begins in slavery and ends in freedom, and whose point of progress at every moment is faith. Specific elements or applications of this walk of faith, such as prayer, the use of possessions, the problems of power, anger and sexuality, evil and suffering, will receive specific attention—not because they are all that deserve consideration, but because they provide solid starting points for the reader's thinking his or her way into other such elements and applications. Also, they are things I have been able to think about. The book ends with a brief evocation of what I consider to be the authentic mark of Christian maturity, the hallmark of the saint, faith's freedom.

Part One

Connections

1

The One with Whom
We Have to Do:
Critical Theological Concepts

God is the Other whom we implicitly encounter when we engage the world. It is of the greatest importance to state from the beginning that what Christians mean by "spirituality" is this encounter with a power and freedom other than, and infinitely greater than, that of humanity itself. The Other is not simply a projection of human fear and desire onto a cosmic screen. Christians do not consider the term God simply a remnant concept, as though God were what was left over when everything else in the world was taken into account. The opposite is true: God is what makes an account of the world possible. When Christians speak of the living God, they mean a power and presence that is more real than their own.

Putting such emphasis on the otherness and realness of God, however, can lead to inappropriate speech. Language shapes as well as reflects our perception. It is important to be critical of our language about God. It is all too easy to identify our *concept* of God with God. We quickly forget that language only partially grasps any reality, and that language about God is necessarily the most inadequate of all. What has traditionally been called negative theology has the role of denying our easy assertions about God, in order to maintain the proper distance between our speech and its referent.

The most prevalent abuse of God-talk is found in the mouths of religious people who speak blithely about God as though the Master of the Universe were a bosom friend. Confident declarations about God's will and God's speaking should be as scandalous to believers as to nonbelievers. Anyone speaking of God who does not remember that God is in heaven and we are on earth is a fool. We cannot talk about God as glibly as we discourse about our neighbors. God is not available for such casual disclosure and manipulation.

Qoheleth sang beautifully that "there is a season and a time for every matter under heaven," but he also declared that God "has made everything beautiful in its time; also he has put eternity into man's mind, yet so that he cannot find out what God has done from the beginning to the end" (Eccles. 3:11). None of us dwelling on earth enjoys sufficient elevation above the mystery of human existence to seize the divine perspective and assert it as our own. We are all in the mire together. We can all therefore confess together that when it comes to God, we simply don't know what it is we are saying. The essential requirement for talk about God is modesty before the Mystery.

It is appropriate, then, to qualify the assertions with which I began. By saying that God is the Other whom we encounter, I do not mean that God is an object among other objects; that God is definable, locatable, controllable. By saying that God is most real, I do not mean to imply that God is most obviously real. By saying that God is power, I do not mean to suggest that God is palpable. And so on, for all bald assertions about God that may occur in this book. The terms Father, Son, and Spirit are metaphors. The use of masculine pronouns for God is conventional, just as would be also the use of feminine pronouns or titles. If we declare that God is wise or good or true, we must hasten to add that God is *not* wise, good, or true in the way people are—granting that we know how people are!

Our language about God consists of pointers to our experience and to our deepest convictions concerning our existence in the world, its origin, shaping and destiny; but at the same time, we affirm that it points beyond our private and even communal experience or conviction to something true. We recognize that our language about God must be circumspect, oblique, moving largely by indirection; denying and qualifying even as it affirms. We both know and do not know. We see in a mirror, indistinctly, but affirm that it is more than our own reflection we discern.

We insist that our language really does point beyond itself. Discourse about God is not utterly meaningless. The proper study of theology is not simply language about God, but the reality of God. To assert, as I have, that we encounter God implicitly in our engagement of the world, is to say a great deal. What is implicit is not less real than what is explicit. In our own everyday experience, we recognize that what is left unsaid can be more important and even more powerful than what is openly stated.

In this connection, the understanding of God as Spirit is critical. The term spirit does not define God adequately. But it helps make clear what is *not* the case with God. We encounter physical things directly and explicitly, body to body. Our encounter with other persons in knowledge and love, however, always has an indirect quality. Our bodies and our speech enable that encounter but do not exhaust it. From the analysis of such interpersonal activities, we conclude that humans in some sense are "spirit." The term spirit describes the necessary condition for knowledge and love. Yet how difficult to state precisely what we mean by that condition as it applies to human knowledge and love! We should therefore be all the more cautious in asserting it for a capacity beyond our everyday world.

Recognizing the limits of our language ought not to render us dumb, only careful. We need not grow so fastidious as to assert only what we can prove or define. Such linguistic agnosticism is inappropriate. I am not able to demonstrate *how* a bumblebee can possibly fly in defiance of physics, but I have in fact seen bumblebees fly, and must state that they can do so. I certainly am not able to prove my existence if you should persistently challenge it, but I am not so silly as on that account to deny my existence. I cannot tell you *why* my wife loves me, but that inadequacy does not lead me to doubt my constant experience of her love for me.

In the Christian creed, there is the same sort of situation. We confess together that "He will come again to judge the living and the dead." At the same time, we must acknowledge that we do not have the slightest clue as to how that might happen. The creed does not explain what it confesses, or reduce the mystery it declares to a set of solvable problems. It is the creed's business to state the convictions that are central to our experience as Christians. Specific interpretations of the creed that have been called heretical within the tradition have been condemned not because anyone was ever in a position satisfactorily to refute them, but because of the communal sense that such heresies either denied or distorted some existential truth.

Within the creed itself some statements are absolutely central to Christian identity. I call such statements critical theological concepts. These are statements for which we are not able adequately to supply the positive content, much less proof of their validity. At the same time, they are statements that are necessary to assert, if we are logically to live in a certain way. The concepts are validated not by facts but by a certain pattern of life. To put it in the shortest possible way, sanctity is itself the most adequate proof for God's existence. In this chapter, I will develop four such critical theological concepts in order to make clear the understanding of God that structures my argument concerning Christian maturity: God as Creator, God as Judge, God as Savior, and God as Sanctifier.

Creator

The statement "God created the heavens and the earth and all that are in them" expresses a conviction *that,* rather than an analysis *how.* It states simply that the visible world is neither self-originated nor independent: the world we inhabit takes its origin from and is ordered to a higher power. The statement does not depend on any specific narrative or theory of world origins. It does not therefore require a scientific reading of the Genesis account. Like the mythologies of all peoples, Genesis expresses existential truths through folk traditions. The statement that God creates the world is perfectly compatible with scientific theories of cosmic chain reactions. The conviction that God creates does not describe one step in such a process, but the primordial cause which underlies and enables the whole process. The further qualification of this basic statement, namely that God created "out of nothing" is meant to indicate that God's activity is not a part of process, still less a piece of it, but is rather its entire premise.

The Christian conviction that God is Creator involves a great deal more than a theory of origins in the chronological sense. It asserts that God continues to create the world at every moment. The world cannot account for itself. It is held out of nothingness by the sustaining and enlivening power of its Creator. Creation is a process that is new every morning. The remarkable consequence of this is that behind every leaf that grows or every wind that blows the presence of God is implicit. Creation reveals God not simply in the form of an architect's plans but primarily in its always surprising *existing* at all, in its ever new and never to be taken for granted coming into being. I encounter God when I engage the world because as the song so succinctly says, "He's got the whole world in his hands." In this perception, the world is a perpetually renewed gift. It is not necessary. It is freely given. And in its being given moment by moment, it reveals—by its very being there— the unseen giver of the gift. Creation is the first gift; it is never withdrawn but neither can it be taken for granted. "Every good endowment and every perfect gift is from above, coming down from the Father of lights with whom there is no variation or shadow due to change" (James 1:17).

God not only creates the world out there, but *my* world at every moment. More than a theory about the world in general is involved. I confess that *I* am held out of nothingness at every moment, that my continuing in being is a gift which never becomes my possession. We do not need elaborate analyses of cosmic forces to prove God's existence and power. The most effective existential proof is to place a finger to one's temple. Feel the thin wall of flesh that separates us from nonbeing. Feel the pulse of life beneath the skin that we can neither control nor perpetuate by our own desire or power. All we need do is acknowledge that we are at every moment a breath away from death, and that the breath we take this moment is a gift we cannot give ourselves.

To deny our utter contingency and our total dependence is willful blindness. If we cannot guarantee even our next breath for ourselves, how can we pretend to control the world? To act as though we were in charge, to presume upon the fact of existence and even to claim it as a possession, is possible only by denying the most obvious of all facts. It is delusion and self-deception. As radically contingent beings, we are at once totally empty and completely filled. We are filled because we do exist, and there is no half-glass of existence. We are empty because all we are comes from an Other by gift and never becomes a possession over which we exercise exclusive control.

Why is the confession of God as Creator a critical theological concept? Because its denial leads to a distorted perception of the world and of our activity within it. To deny creation is to assert that there is nothing beyond the world. However it came into being, the world is a closed system. It neither reflects an Other's intelligence and will, nor discloses any meaning aside from those we assign it. Such a perception makes all the world's inhabitants into competitors for survival. If being is not a gift from a Creator, then it is a possession to be acquired. In a closed system, there is only so much being to go around. We are players in a zero-sum game: I can be more only if you are less; I thrive at your expense. The ideal of a brotherhood or sisterhood of humans that is not based in the fatherhood or motherhood of a Creator is either a romantic fantasy, or a desperate strategy.

The statement that God creates the world is in the most proper sense a radical statement. It expresses the most important truth about reality and about our human lives. Every other assertion about God and about the human encounter with God derives from and depends on this first truth: that a power and life greater than we could ever imagine presses upon us in every circumstance of our lives, at once gifting us and calling us. Likewise, the denial of God as Creator is also the most fundamental lie, distorting every perception of the world and every engagement with it. It is a lie, furthermore, that forecloses other truth.

If the acknowledgement of God as creator is the opening of our eyes to a light that enables us to see all things clearly in their proper order and therefore in their luminous beauty, so the refusal to acknowledge our own and the world's origin from God is a deliberate blindness that causes us to stumble through a world of darkness, losing our way and our very selves.

Judge

No article of the creed is so regularly denied or distorted as this one: "He will come again to judge the living and the dead." The denials are based at least in part on the distortions. An over-emphasis on apocalyptic by milennarian Christians, with a particular fixation on its Armageddon aspects, cannot but cause disgust among the more balanced. When all thought and effort is focused on the timing of the rapture and whether we will be aboard, Christian identity itself is distorted. Partly in reaction to such over-emphasis, and partly because of a perspective on the world shaped by modernity, many other Christians have entirely removed God's judgment from their religious lexicon. Because of this polarization, it is both necessary and difficult to state the conviction that God is Judge. Yet it is integral to the Christian creed.

It may be helpful to begin with the causes of this polarization in Christian consciousness. We have learned a great deal in recent years about the social sources of milennarian expectation. The expectation of divine retribution has obvious appeal to those who are oppressed. The marginalized within a society, especially those who lack possessions, power, or prestige commensurate with their expectations, find a deep resonance in the theme of a Judge who will rectify this state of affairs. If we are the righteous, and the righteous are presently being eclipsed, then it makes sense that we will long for a divine leveling, a cosmic reversal.

In contemporary fundamentalist Christianity, the obsessive clinging to an apocalyptic mythology owes something as well to the experience of being intellectually marginalized. If the conviction that Jesus will return to judge the world is the belief that is most rejected and scorned by intellectuals, and if we regard them as godless anyway, then the greatest symbol of our dedication to God's truth is a firm commitment to this reviled expectation for a new heaven and a new earth, with all the tribulation that precedes them.

But on the other side, why have the intellectuals either rejected this article of the creed or so drastically reinterpreted it as to leave it unrecognizable? More is involved than the cosmetic emphasis within some communities on a loving God as opposed to a judging God. More is involved than a dismissal of a mythological imaging of God's judgment in terms of a Great Assize. More is involved even than the age-old dismay at the triumph of evil in the world. This is not the first generation to experience a cognitive dissonance between the plain facts and our dearest convictions: no matter how much we protest that God punishes the wicked and rewards the good, we see no visible evidence of it. The oppressors wax strong; the oppressed cry out in vain.

The elimination of the concept of judgment has, I think, happened this way: the conviction that God is Judge of the world derives from the prior conviction that God creates the world. God not only brings the world into being at every moment, not only sustains it by power, but orders it by intelligence and rules it by will. God has Creator's knowledge of the world, more intimate than which cannot be imagined; the world's teleology is God's will. In the most profound sense, therefore, the world is answerable to God. But if God is not Creator of the world in this sense, then there can be no real meaning to the belief that God is Judge. The loss of eschatology follows the loss of a Creator.

Precisely the elimination of the Creator characterizes the perception of the world we call modernity: We are alone in the world. The cosmos may be a garden, but we cannot prove it has a gardener. We may perhaps find the symbol "God" helpful as an articulation of our hopes, or even as the cutting edge of our human social project. God at best is in process of becoming God through the human projects of evolution and revolution. But God is not the Other who is powerfully present before and beneath those processes. God is not the Being above being who calls into existence that which is not and therefore poses a question to all existing things for which God alone is the only adequate answer. Such a conceptual God cannot judge because this God has no life or power to give life. This God indeed is mere projection.

To confess God as Judge, however, does not mean that we claim to know *how* God judges. The Christian is as thoroughly in the dark as anyone else, observes with the same anguish the suffering of the just and the arrogance of the wicked. The Christian cannot supply the positive content of this confession, having no more direct information than the unbeliever on heaven or hell, and no better evidence for their existence. But the believer insists that this confession has less to do with a visible *how* than with an invisible *that*. Our confession does not define the manner in which God restores right relations among humans, but asserts as present reality that God knows rightly what those relations are. The heart of this critical theological concept is that God is the discerner of the heart.

By declaring that God is judge the Christian means first that God is *our* Judge here and now. All we think and say and do lies bare before the all-seeing eye of God. Although we may be opaque to each other, we are transparent to our Creator. God knows us utterly as we are. God knows us rightly at every moment. In every encounter between humans—and between humans and the world—the total truth of that encounter is held only by its unseen enabler. And more: at every moment of my life, even when I am most alone, I am transparent to my Creator, my heart is open to God's discernment, I am known more completely and truly by God than I know myself.

A contemporary thinker has complained that "the stare" of other people reduces us to an object. The Christian confession of God as judge asserts precisely the opposite. To be known (seen) in this fashion by the one who is truly Other establishes us as a subject. It provides us with the very basis for our freedom to be ourselves, rather than the prisoner of the perceptions of other people. It is because we are open to the gaze of the Other that we can afford to be honest with ourselves. We let ourselves admit what is already known to the One who counts. It is because God is judge that our interior intentions count; purity of heart is significant only if the intentions of the heart are being judged.

What follows when we deny the confession that God judges the world? First, we must assume the entire responsibility for justice being done in the world. If God is powerless to reward the just and punish the wicked, then we must do it. And since we have no heaven or hell, we must do it now. Vengeance is not only legitimated, it is demanded. Yet, tragically, we lack the necessary capacity to do justice, for we do not see all things and see them truly. We do not understand the workings of our own heart much less those of others. We can observe only the surfaces of things, and must therefore judge by appearances, which is exactly the way Scripture characterizes corrupt judgment (see Lev. 19:15)! We are placed in the impossible situation of bearing a divine responsibility while having only human capacity. The declaration "Vengeance is mine, I will repay, says the Lord" (Deut. 32:35; Rom. 12:19) does not tell us how it will be accomplished. But it does protect humans from a terrible responsibility they are incapable of fulfilling.

The denial that God is Judge distorts even more intimate truths. Why should we care about the sincerity of our intentions and motivations, if they are not known by One who discerns correctly and without bias? With one stroke, the collapse of our conviction concerning God as Judge causes to fall as well the reason for interiority. Why be sincere, if all that can be observed is appearance? If all that counts is joining the right cause or performing the right actions—and what else could count, if my only judges are my fellow dim-sighted humans—then why should I not be hypocritical? What possible meaning could there be to the prayer of silence if there is not an Other before whom my heart lies bare?

If God is not the One who gifts us with being at every moment and in the same action calls us by name—that is, knows us as we are and challenges us to the acceptance of the truth about ourselves— if God is only a cosmic process powerless apart from the cooperation of humans, then God cannot judge. And we cannot be truly known. Or ever truly accepted.

Savior

To name God as our Savior means of course that we relinquish the title for ourselves. We assert our absolute and continuing dependence on the One who creates us. Neither our cunning nor our courage can establish us in being. We remain always receivers. And what we have received can never be transmuted to a possession completely within our control, still less a basis from which to control God.

What are we saved from? Since all that exists comes by gift from God, we are not saved from the visible world or some part of it. Salvation does not mean shedding our bodies to preserve our souls. Rather, salvation involves all that we are, both physical and spiritual. It is sin we need saving from. Sin is a derangement of our freedom and a distortion of our relationship to reality—first of all to the Creator. Salvation therefore means, in negative terms, release from the imprisonment of sin, and thereby liberation from death and the fear of death.

This brings us to the more profound sense of salvation in the Christian tradition. Salvation is not only a liberation *from* but a freedom *for*. The Creator abounds in life and wishes to share it fully with creatures. The distinctive gift given to humans is a capacity to receive that fuller life of God. This gift we call grace. It lifts us beyond ourselves into the most intimate of relationships with God, a share in God's own eternal life. The expectation of sharing in the life of God, of dwelling in that powerful presence of God called glory is expressed by our hope in the resurrection of the dead and in the life of the world to come.

I pause here and remind myself and my reader that each of these concepts is laden with complex associations. Each of them is capable of infinite study and amplification. Yet I tick them off, sentence by sentence! I can justify this partly because each of these ideas is going to recur repeatedly and with greater nuance in later chapters. My only purpose here is to get the framework down as briskly as possible. Indeed, no amount of qualification will make the concepts any more plausible or congenial. We may as well get the whole dose down at once.

Think for a moment, though, how shocking the statements I have been making are to the two models of Christian spirituality I have sketched. The gnostic model prefers to think of God as inhabiting the higher reaches of the human soul; what is needed is escape from the clutches of the body and its passions. The liberation model hopes to find God realized in the egalitarian structures of future society. If for one model the thought of a future for the body seems impossible, for the other the hope for eternal life seems fantastic. Nor is the Christian unaware of the problems created by these bold assertions. Bodies, after all, die and rot in the earth. We know that! We can also see that the alternative models offer more logical eschatologies: we can either save souls eternally or bodies temporally. But Christians insist on the impossible paradox: saving bodies eternally. Nowhere is it more necessary for us to repeat that we assert what we do not fully understand, that we confess what we can neither satisfactorily describe nor adequately define, much less prove to anyone's satisfaction, even our own.

On what basis, then, do we insist on this peculiar and paradoxical understanding of salvation? On the basis of our experience of God in Jesus Christ, whom we also designate as our Savior. The Christian confession that God's Word became incarnate in Jesus has implications for more than the singular historical person Jesus. It means that the human capacity to receive fully the gift of God's presence has been realized completely, so that if by the perfect communication of gift and acceptance one among us can be called Son of God, all of us can thereby measure what it means to be "children of God." In Jesus, both God's self-donation in knowledge and love and the human ability to accept that gift are realized. The Incarnation is God's complete embrace of creation. Because the "Word became flesh" all of material reality bears the impress of Spirit and of Life.

The Incarnation means more than the "fact" of God's taking on our humanity. It means as well God's involvement with the full human story of a specific historical man's life, death, and resurrection. The center of our creed bristles with hard pieces of historical fact, "born of the virgin Mary, suffered under Pontius Pilate, crucified, died, and buried." The incarnation means therefore God's assumption of the human narrative, from birth to death. Just as by God's taking on a body all materiality is dignified and never to be despised, so by the living out of one singular human story from beginning to end, does God render all human stories potential sources of divine revelation. The assertion of early Christian teachers that "what is not assumed cannot be saved" accurately states the central conviction—based on the fact of Jesus—that God has saved the world by becoming totally involved with the world.

In the confession, "He rose again on the third day," we discover the most paradoxical element in the Christian affirmation of God as Savior. It might be possible to think of the Incarnation as a straightforward validation of human existence as such, or, even to conclude that some part of humans is already divine. The confession of a crucified and raised Messiah shatters such fantasies. God's gift of life is the gift of *new* life, not simply the continuation of the old. Grace is not a slight improvement but a totally new possibility. Glory is not simply more of what we have but something else altogether. Nothing could more dramatically state what we believe about God as Creator than the resurrection of Jesus. He truly died and truly was buried. But God on the third day raised him to new life. As free gift.

It is not simply the emergence of new leaves every spring after the literal death of winter, or the appearance of the sun every morning after the literal death of night (for these are certainly more than metaphor), that ground our conviction that God's creation is always and everywhere out of nothing and that the gift of life and power is given freely by One who is Other than the world and the basis of the world's being. Our conviction is based directly on the resurrection of Jesus.

Nothing in our experience is more real than death, and nothing more final. When we confess therefore that one has died and has entered by the gift of God into a new and still more powerful form of existence, indeed lives now as Lord at the right hand of the Father, then we emphatically assert that the One with whom we have to do is beyond our control or comprehension, is the Holy One. Paul, speaking of the righteousness of Abraham, refers to "the God in whom he believed, the God who gives life to the dead and calls into existence the things that do not exist"; and adds that the righteousness attributed to Abraham also "will be reckoned to us who believe in him that raised from the dead Jesus our Lord, who was put to death for our trespasses and raised for our justification" (Rom. 4:17, 24-25).

God as Savior is therefore truly manifested to us through the life, death, and resurrection of Jesus. Essential to the Christian confession is this truth: The story of Jesus shows us who God is. The entire Christian soteriology, in turn, is based on a Messiah who was not only born human and died (as do all humans), but who was executed as a criminal and was then raised to a new and more powerful existence by God. It is in the light of the resurrection of Jesus that we define Christian cosmology and anthropology and eschatology, simply because it is in the death and resurrection of

Jesus that we have had the distinctive and constitutive experience of salvation.

Because of Jesus our eschatology is a hope for the resurrection of the dead and the life of the world to come, no matter how logical other eschatologies may sound. We cannot assert only the salvation of the soul apart from the body, for we confess that the body of Jesus continues to mediate his powerful presence to the world. Do we understand how we could have *any* life beyond death, much less how we might be embodied in God's life? Certainly not. We confess what we cannot define or prove, because to deny it would be to deny our own experience. But on the other hand, neither can we envisage the life of the world to come in terms of the (slightly improved) structures of the present world, or define our hope simply as long life, children, and possession of the land, with equality, solidarity, and liberty. Why? Because the new life offered by God in Jesus does not consist in those things, but in the resurrection of the body, a sharing in the very life of God.

In our experience of Jesus, we have not only learned how God seeks solidarity with creation and friendship with humans. We have learned as well how humans can accept God's gift. Jesus is at once the "Yes" of God to the world, and the "Yes" of the world to God in return (2 Cor. 1:20). In the narrative of this singular human being of the first century Mediterranean world, who bore in himself the explicit burden of the world's drama, played out elsewhere only implicitly and in shadow, we find the fundamental narrative of God's dealings with us, and ours with God. From the side of God we learn that the gift of life can be mediated through bodily presence: "since the children share in flesh and blood, he himself likewise partook of the same nature" (Heb. 2:14). From the side of humanity, we learn that the acceptance of God's gift can take place in the specific and homely structures of ordinary life: "He who sanctifies and those who are sanctified have all one origin. That is why he is not ashamed to call them brethren" (Heb. 2:11).

Jesus is therefore not simply the "cause of our salvation" (Heb. 5:9) whom Christians confess in faith as Lord; he is also our brother, whose faith in God we share. Because God assumed full humanity and not just a body, God entered into an exchange of gift and acceptance with human freedom. In Jesus, we find the proper expression of human freedom, the expression of "perfected humanity." Jesus is the "pioneer and perfecter of faith" (Heb. 12:2), the model of how human faith works.

Christians instinctively, properly, and carefully consider the path Jesus walked as a human being. They study the manner in which Jesus is the way to God, the truth about humanity, the expression of God's life in the world (cf. John 14:6), and seek to understand the teaching, "No one comes to the Father, but by me," not in terms of a narrow doctrinal commitment, but in this sense: no one can enter into friendship with God except in the manner Jesus has done, and no one could possibly follow that manner except by "the new and living way which he opened for us . . . through his flesh" (Heb. 10:19).

The specific *Christian* spirituality, then, is one that is centered on the experience of God as Savior through Jesus. We acknowledge that the gift of life, of peace, of reconciliation, and of righteousness, comes through the crucified and resurrected Messiah. And in the messianic pattern enacted by Jesus' life and death, we recognize as well the model for our own acceptance of that gift. In every situation, our instinct is to "look to Jesus," (Heb 12:2). From beginning to end, the form of Christian spirituality is the imitation of Christ.

Sanctifier

We come now to the part of the creed perhaps most immediately pertinent to our argument, for when we speak of the Holy Spirit, we touch on the transforming power by which God touches and transforms us. The word "Holy" is most properly used only of God. It designates the Otherness of God. God is different than the world, or anything in the world. God is not controllable by any human concept or desire but is sovereign freedom. Perhaps the most astonishing assertion placed by Scripture in God's mouth is this one: "Be holy, for I am holy" (Lev. 11:44). It is reasserted by Paul, "This is the will of God, your sanctification" (1 Thess. 4:3). What God essentially is, God wills that we should become. To translate this as directly as possible, as God is different *from* the world, we are intended to be different *within* the world.

The meaning of this difference can of course be endlessly debated. Does it consist in keeping a set of rules that demarcates one people from others in terms of diet and ritual? Is it a matter of social policy or ideology or even social structures that distinguish us from others? The classic answer to this question within Christianity is straightforward and unequivocal: the difference comes from the transformation of persons by the Spirit. It is not simply a matter of human awareness or decision, but of the human response to God's gift. The gift and the reception both are enabled by the Spirit. As Paul continues, "God has not called us for uncleanness, but in holiness. Therefore whoever disregards this, disregards not man but God, who gives his Holy Spirit to you" (1 Thess. 4:7-8).

Sanctity, or holiness, is therefore appropriately considered the goal of Christian existence. The mature Christian is the saint. The symbol we use for the power by which God effects this transformation of human consciousness and freedom is the Holy Spirit. Spirituality therefore means the whole process of gift and response by which God carves out a space for God's freedom in the human heart.

Distinctive to Christian spirituality is the conviction that the Spirit has been made available, indeed powerfully present in the world, through the resurrection of Jesus. Jesus was, Paul tells us, "designated Son of God in power according to the Spirit of holiness by his resurrection from the dead" and therefore it is "through him" that we have received grace and apostleship (Rom. 1:5). In contrast to Adam who became a "living being," says Paul, Jesus by his resurrection became "life-giving Spirit" (1 Cor. 15:45). Jesus is not only the source of the Spirit. Jesus provides as well the shape of the Spirit's work. The pattern of transformation is given in the life and death of the Messiah himself. The work of sanctification is therefore the work of replicating in the lives of Christians the messianic pattern enacted by God in Jesus. The way he went is the way we are to go. The power and the direction alike are provided by the Holy Spirit. This is what Paul means when he says, "if we live by the Spirit let us also walk by the Spirit," and when he adds shortly thereafter, "thus fulfill the law of Christ" (Gal. 5:25; 6:2), which is to say, "thus enact in your own life the pattern of the Messiah."

Exactly what this pattern of the Messiah is, and how it can be enacted in the diversity and confusion of everyday life will preoccupy us throughout this book. The nature of the pattern itself is not arcane. It is clearly imprinted in the narratives of the Gospel. The Gospels, however, relate the particulars of a first century Jewish teacher. Distinguishing the pattern from the particulars takes some effort. How does the radical faith and self-emptying love of that historical person get translated into a paradigm for all persons? The translation process began already in the composition of those narratives, for they were written by and for Christians whose lives had already been transformed by the Spirit of Jesus and it was in the light of that experience that they shaped these narratives of God's Son. The process of translation continues, however, in every reader of those narratives, not only in the way each reader construes the narrative, but in the way the narrative constructs each reader.

If the work of the Spirit is to replicate in our lives the story of Jesus, certain components of Christian spirituality immediately are suggested. Christian perfection cannot be sought solely in the performance of specific deeds without the transformation of the heart in faith and love. The actual deeds of Jesus are mostly unrepeatable; the direction of his freedom, which generated those actions, is, however, renewable in the hearts of others. Transformation begins with the "renewal of our minds" (Rom. 12:2) and the "purity of our hearts" (James 4:8). At the same time, Christian perfection cannot remain a matter of mind or attitude. The faith and love of Jesus was enacted in specific engagements with his world, above all with his fellow humans. So also must Christian spirituality include the physical and the social dimensions of life.

Despite the incapacity of our language to speak appropriately about God, it is necessary to say some things in order to protect the integrity of our experience of the world. I have tried to sketch briefly four such "critical concepts" about God, using the classic Christian understanding of God as Creator, Judge, Savior, and Sanctifier as a way of locating my argument concerning the shape of Christian perfection, or maturity. No matter how hard I try to translate these terms into everyday language, they remain elusive and remote. They still state much more what I am supposed to think rather than what I do think or feel about my life. In order to translate these theological terms more adequately into the speech of everyday experience, then, we need to take an equally long look at the junior partners in this divine drama. We need to look carefully at the structures and systems of our human existence. Just what is it we mean when we talk about the human project in the world?

2

The Human Project:
Freedom and Its Conditions

What is man that thou art mindful of him, and the son of man that thou dost care for him?" (Ps. 8:4). The question of the psalmist is not easily answered, yet if we are to make the life of the Spirit intelligible we must at least examine the question's implications. In this chapter, then, I turn to an examination of the human project. Just as certain theological concepts are necessary to maintain the internal coherence of the Christian confession, so are certain anthropological concepts necessary for a coherent vision of Christian existence in the world.

A word on the spirit of this inquiry. If I find the psalmist's phrasing of the question appropriate, I obviously think from the start that humans have someone mindful of them and caring for them. I make no pretense, therefore, of developing an anthropology that is not already essentially shaped by the narrative of faith. But neither am I simply constructing an elaborate make-believe question to which God is the predetermined answer.

The task here is to describe the human role in the drama of faith. The difficulties of such description are obvious; the dangers both of oversimplification and obfuscation are real. Even raising the questions runs the risk of deflecting the argument: Why do I define freedom this way? Why do I use the terms I do? My interest, however, is not so much theoretical as practical. I want to establish a common understanding of what it means when we talk about human experience, and some basic and important things can be said. Disagreements or conclusions are often based in a fundamental confusion about what the facts are or how things work. What follows, therefore, is my perception of what's going on in our shared human existence, my list of critical anthropological concepts for an adequate analysis of Christian spirituality.

When speaking about God, I observed that no one can seize the divine perspective and make it one's own. A similar caution is required when speaking about the human condition. No one stands outside it as an objective observer, capable of cooly reducing the ambiguities of human life to a neat set of equations. Every statement about humanity implicates the human being who makes the statement. As with language about God, caution and circumspection are appropriate.

The Gift and Task of Freedom

The most important thing to say about humans is that they are free. The flat statement contains obvious problems. The ways individuals and social groups are limited in their freedom are easy to enumerate. By no means is each act performed by a human being undetermined. In fact, freedom of choice as a quality of specific decisions is not the most significant aspect of freedom. At this point, rather, I am using freedom as the appropriate way to describe the peculiarly human predicament.

Human freedom can be defined negatively in terms of instinctual impoverishment. Humans do not follow imprinted patterns as do other animals; they do not migrate seasonally or molt. Bears look and act like bears wherever they appear. By comparison, humans are undetermined. They appear almost infinitely adaptable. They can be carnivorous or vegetarian; clothed or unclothed; alone or in groups. Precisely their capacity to adapt to a wide variety of environments indicates their lack of a rigid instinctual control. It is possible to be human in a bewildering variety of ways. Human behavior is not determined solely by biological necessities. To take only the most intriguing example, mating among animals is rigidly governed by fertility cycles. But humans can mate at will, abstain from sexual activity despite the urging of their hormones, or arrange themselves in inventive sexual combinations.

The fact of cultural pluralism strongly supports the suggestion that human nature does not reside in a set of behaviors that make up a self, but in the capacity to create a self according to a number of different patterns. The best way to describe the human animal may be in terms of indeterminacy, as an existent, sentient, conscious being that is in the process of becoming a human person. This process of becoming person is the project of human freedom.

Although humans at birth are not automatically provided a single center for their activity, they retain as their most characteristic "instinct" the overwhelming need to find or create such a center. The paradox of human freedom is that it does not seem to be able to function when undirected. Total liberty strikes terror in the heart, a sense of complete contingency paralyzes action. We seem to be so constructed as to require something to be necessary or all-important or absolute, even though we are impressively capricious in selecting what it will be. We are all presented a number of convincing candidates. Our physical and social environments offer plausible reasons for being considered centers for the human project of becoming a person.

The process of becoming a self demands a stage of gaining "freedom from" the counterfeit claimants to necessity and real being. That is hard enough. But worse is the stage of positively directing one's freedom. If the center that enables us to become self is not found here or there, in this or that, where is it found? And, if it is found, how can we relate ourselves to that which is truly necessary, and still be free?

This perilous path of freedom is enabled—indeed required—by the fact of human consciousness. It is because we are, however partially, spirit, that we are open-ended projects in the world, always unfinished this side of death, always capable of change. We do not need to locate this spirit either in brain or soul in order to assert its reality. We know that we are spirit because we can engage the world in knowledge and love.

Purely physical entities can unite only by physical closeness. By knowledge and intention, I can inhabit or be inhabited by another no matter how far our bodies are separated. We can press our hands together as long as we want but they will not merge: We can glue stones together as tightly as possible; time will pull them apart and reveal them for what they always were: two objects artificially joined. But by spirit we can walk within each other's heads and hearts even when physically absent. We can, by spirit, get inside. By spirit, we engage the world as a project for the self. Is this real? Yes, it is real. I need only listen to a Mozart concerto to understand everything that is necessary to know about spirit and its transcendence. The man who picks up my garbage inhabits the same space I do once a week, but if I do not know him or love him, he is merely another object in the world. Mozart leaps across the centuries, across notes on pages, across catgut and wood, and springs into my mind and heart, and enlarges my world. Mozart, indeed, continues to become self in his enacted music, just as I grow into my self when his music enters and moves me.

From our capacity to know and love across space and time, we conclude that we are spirit. Spirit makes us subjects who can engage the world as other, but also penetrate that world and make it part of our own self. It is because we have the capacity to perceive and change perception, to choose and to alter choices, that we are otherwise instinctually impoverished. All other beings have a home in the world; oaks remain always oaks, dolphins stay dolphins. Consciousness opens human beings to freedom with all its perils and possibilities.

The perils are real and the possibilities are not infinite. To speak realistically about the project of human freedom means speaking as well about the ways that freedom is conditioned and constrained. I will discuss in turn the physical, psychological, sociological and hermeneutical dimensions of our human project. In each case, I provide the merest sketch. I want only to indicate the way each dimension limits but also makes definite the direction of freedom, as well as the way each dimension represents another aspect of the world within which the human project is shaped.

Physical Dimensions — Holds a very dualistic view of spirit/body

Nothing puts so obvious a constraint on our freedom as the fact that we have and are bodies. The complex relationship to ourselves, others, and the world that is established by bodiliness will be touched on in later discussions of power and possessions and sexuality. For now, we can simply remind ourselves of the ways in which the human spirit is fettered by the flesh. Our bodily existence is fragile and subject to multiple embarrassments both in youth and in age. Our capacity to see clearly and choose wisely is constantly threatened by our physical cravings and revulsions. We need not regard the body as evil to recognize that it encumbers the spirit. The body requires tending for the spirit to function. The body's appetites cannot be ignored without peril. In the most obvious way, our bodies demand attention. It is difficult to contemplate truth when the stomach growls with hunger.

Above all, because we are bodies we can inhabit only one place in the world at a time, and we can dispose of our freedom only one moment at a time. No matter how global our vision or grand our desire, we can never roll our freedom into a ball, throw it one way or another, and be done with it. Our choices, like our steps, must follow one another in sequence. Even if our spirit leaps for an instant in ecstasy, it must return to the stumbling pace of the everyday world. Because we are bodies in time, we suffer. Our spirit may wish to act, but our bodies may be able only to endure. Sickness, aging, and death are the inevitable destiny of bodies.

All this is true. Yet because we are also more than simply somatic, we can exercise freedom with regard to our own bodies. We cannot remove ourselves from time, but we can transcend time both by memory and by hope. We cannot occupy more than one place in the world, but we can imagine every other place. We cannot utterly destroy desire and fear, but we can relativize their power. We are not forced to eat when we are hungry, even when food is placed before us. We can fast for repentance or for the hungry poor. We are creatures of sexual desire, but we need not consummate every lust; we can be celibate. We cannot choose whether to experience anger, for it is biologically determined, but we can choose the expression of anger. We cannot eliminate physical sickness and pain altogether, but we can choose the attitude we take to our sickness and pain.

Our bodies specify the exercise of our freedom, and limit its range. But they also enable the expression of our spirit in the world. Because of my body, I can occupy only one place at a time; but because of my body, I can also transform this place, at this moment. Through our bodies we engage the world and each other. As bodies we touch and gaze into each other's eyes and know with a knowing that does not require words. But also as bodies we speak and listen, taste and savor, touch and caress, strive and struggle, lift and liberate, change and give growth. Our bodies are the primordial symbols of our spirit; they extend our freedom into the world; they enable encounter and change; they incarnate our project of selfhood.

Our bodies, indeed, are so impressively present and imperious in their demands that freedom can fixate on their service. Our spirit can choose to limit itself to the upkeep and maintenance of the body: its health, beauty, longevity, pleasure, possessions, power. It is possible for our freedom to aim so low: to make the avoidance of physical pain and the comfort of the body its total project. The self, it might be decided, *is* simply the body, nothing more. Therefore, the body's appearance needs constant tending, its appetites require catering, its cravings demand satisfaction. But since discomfort, physical pain and suffering are the inevitable concomitants of bodily existence, the only total treatment lies in the dulling of the body's capacity to feel anything. The logic of centering in the body is spelled out in addiction. The drugging of the body anesthetizes the spirit so it will not see how narrow is its prison.

Psychological Dimensions

The development of depth psychology has revealed within us an underworld of emotional complexity that ancient people never suspected. We have learned, for example, that fear and desire and anger can operate powerfully outside our awareness or conscious control. Indeed, we have found that the conscious and unconscious realms are engaged in tense dialogue throughout our lives. When powerful emotions are denied or repressed, they can find expression in patterns of obsession and compulsion that severely limit our freedom. Awareness of these unconscious psychic energies and the mechanisms by which we deny or direct them is important for the proper assessment of human freedom. We can no longer blithely assume that our conscious intentions or motivations are the sole determinants of our actions. On the other hand, neither should we conclude that we are utterly captive to unseen psychic forces. Degrees of debility are recognized even by the most deterministic psychology: psychosis renders one unfree much more profoundly than does neurosis. The very practice of psychological therapy, furthermore, rests on the premise that the knowledge of causes can create some freedom from their effects.

The importance of the emotions for an adequate model of spirituality can scarcely be overemphasized. Their importance is not confined to the fact that because they are rooted in our bodies emotions cannot safely be ignored any more than we can neglect our bodies without peril. Their importance is not found simply in the way we all find ourselves in a struggle between what we ought and what we want, and grow confused about or even collapse the distinction between the two. Nor are the emotions critical because, like the apostle Paul, we sometimes must acknowledge "I do not do what I want, but I do the very thing I hate" (Rom. 7:15). Finally, the importance of emotions certainly does *not* lie in their capacity to direct our actions wisely; knowing what we feel does not prescribe what we are to do.

Nevertheless, knowing what we feel is an essential aspect of making responsible choices. Why? Because emotions are the truest indicators of what is going on in our hearts. In our heads, we are capable of the most elaborate self-justifications, rationalizations and pep-talks. But our stomachs do not lie: the lurch of fear and anxiety, the spasm of dread, the surge of desire; these are not wise, but they are true. The emotions serve a critical diagnostic function for free-dom. When they are unattended and denied, they can mutely and stubbornly move us as captives, against our will. But when they are allowed to speak, they contribute to the dialogue of discernment that is the mark of mature freedom.

The contemporary appreciation of the emotions deriving from depth psychology does not contradict but complements a more traditional understanding of psychology that focuses on freedom as the formation of character. In this traditional understanding, humans become themselves (shape their character) bit by bit. Each choice has an effect not only in the world but in the soul, because we are creatures of *habit*. The choices we make form patterns, provide the basis for subsequent choices. Our freedom is found not simply in a series of random choices, but precisely in the formation of the patterns which incrementally form a self. Depth psychology, in turn, reminds us that these choices are not always made at the level of full consciousness, that some of our most fundamental choices, indeed, precede our coming to awareness of them. We can, quite literally, slip into one kind of character or another.

This is so fundamental and important a point that we should pause over it. We misconceive our freedom when we imagine it as a free-floating decision machine, equally capable at every moment of going in one direction or another. Our prior decisions deeply affect our subsequent decisions, because they facilitate one choice over another. The first time I am violent, I may have to overcome enormous internal resistance formed by my many years of non-violence. But once I have done violence, my next act of violence will be easier. Habit greases the skids. Bit by bit,without my knowing it, I can become a violent person, for whom the exercise of force is always and automatically the first expression of character. How does this happen? There is much in it that is mysterious. But *that* it happens is of the greatest importance. Our freedom is not entirely contained in any single decision we make. But every decision we make is significant for the direction of our freedom. Our choices simultaneously express and form our selves.

Just as our bodies limit our freedom yet also enable its expression, so do our emotions. They can inhibit free choice, but they also play a critical role in making free choice. In turn, our choices condition our emotions. We become habituated to choices in one direction rather than another, simply because it feels right so to do.

And as we can make the survival or comfort of our bodies the project of our freedom, so also can we make our goal the equilibrium of our emotions. In the ancient world, the condition called *apatheia* (freedom from feeling) or *ataraxia* (freedom from disturbance) was some philosophers' goal. The ideal was perfect tranquillity; whatever could threaten emotional balance was eliminated. In the contemporary world, various health therapies have remarkably similar goals: stress management and relaxation techniques are their benign manifestations. Apathy in the face of human need and suffering are less attractive extensions of the same outlook. If emotional equilibrium is an ultimate good, much of the experience of the world must be excluded. This vision of perfection requires a consuming preoccupation with one's own feelings and the neglect of the feelings of others.

However valuable and important emotional health may be, we recognize that there is something terribly truncated and even sad about people who make it their total project. We recognize in them the tendency of human freedom to premature closure, to identifying a real but limited good with ultimate good. And in such closure, we recognize as well a kind of imprisonment. Health, even when measured by psychic efficiency, is not the same thing as sanctity; and sickness, even that of emotional dysfunction or derangement, is not the same thing as sin.

Social Dimensions

Humans are essentially social creatures. Our freedom therefore intersects the freedom of other people. My project of becoming a person inevitably encounters other humans with such projects of their own. None of us is born into a world consisting only of ourselves and nature. We are born into already formed societies, with complex structures and systems of interaction and symbolic undergirding. We must negotiate the structures and roles established before our arrival, which dictate in considerable detail the procedures by which humans shall arrange themselves in family, club, city, and state; how they shall perform the roles required of those respective structures; and how their success or failure shall be measured. Each human is presented at birth with a set of selves as real as a wardrobe of clothes.

The most obvious effect of society on an individual's freedom is the way it limits it. Since we ourselves did not create the world of social structures and symbols into which we are born, it appears to us as natural and even as necessary. Society preserves itself by imprinting in our minds and actions its myths and rituals. So subtle yet powerful is this process that it takes great effort even to become aware of it. A society's values become ours in a process of socialization that begins with birth. What we perceive as appropriate and as good, or shameful and ugly, derives from the perceptions given us by the stories and practices of our culture. It is the easiest, most natural thing in the world to let our freedom run on the grooves already greased by custom.

It is a relief not to have to make choices because my group has already made them for me. Am I an academic? I need not worry any more about my political preference, my taste in clothes, my choice of a mate, my selection of friends, my allocation of resources. These are determined for me, with an amazingly precise calibration, by the customary usages of the caste called academia, down to the leather patches on my tweed coats. The precedents established by custom are powerful and difficult to resist, even in cultures as defined by pluralism as those in which we now live. Indeed, it could be argued that when consensus about the values of society as a whole is not available, the demands of conformity within each subgroup tend to be even stronger.

The great benefit of a self given by societal custom is that it frees us from having to negotiate every encounter as though it were new or unique; we are given roles and procedures to govern our interactions. These keep us from doing violence to one another, and they free our minds for the points that do require attention and negotiation. The great danger of custom is that we can easily allow our self to be only the one dictated by society. We can become nothing more than a bearer of tradition. I never have to think about my self because my self is given in the societal expectations for my various roles of son, husband, teacher, friend, priest. This is a danger because society's implicit claim to ultimacy is only a matter of expediency for its own survival. Society must pretend to be necessary in order to exist at all. It is in fact a very useful fiction. Most of us would agree that civilization is preferable to chaos. But to naively consider the norms or authority of any specific human society as ultimate is to place myself in the most profound alienation from my own project to become a person. Freedom falls short when it submits entirely to custom.

Our historical perspective on all the different kinds of societies that existed in the past and our awareness of all the cultural combinations existing today have forced on us an appreciation of society unavailable to earlier people who knew only their own culture. We see now that no single society can claim to be the perfect norm for all humans. It is natural for humans to arrange themselves in groups, but no particular kind of group is self-evidently natural and necessary. Rather, we have come to see societies as creations of human knowledge and will. We have come to see that customs are rigid because they are inherently fragile; to work at all, they depend on our agreement that they are real and even necessary. If our consensus fails, so also do our customs. More than any other generation, it seems, we have a sense of the customary as the arbitrary. Our most fundamental perception of the social world is that it is changeable.

This perception frees us but also places us in a peculiarly perilous position. On the one hand, we can no more do without the structures and systems of society than any age before us; we, too, need myths and rituals enabling us to live together without violence or waste of energy. On the other hand, we cannot be persuaded that our tattered myths and rituals are ultimate or necessary; we are too well aware of other arrangements and other stories. We are caught, in other words, between alienation and anomie. We can submerge ourselves in our particular social world, pretending to ourselves that it is all that it claims to be, and thus become strangers to our selves. Or we can reject our society's norms as arbitrary, and thereby experience another sort of estrangement, the free-floating anxiety that accompanies the complete lack of structure or law.

The tension of which I speak is experienced most acutely by intellectuals. Their learning makes them acutely aware of pluralism as a factor, not only for others, but above all for themselves. Many intellectuals experience a frightening sense of being uprooted. Their minds expand to cover all cultures and plausibility structures and methods and paradigms; but they have nowhere to place their own feet. Increasingly, they find it difficult to act at all, so relative do all values appear. Intellectuals find it impossible to abandon such awareness and, in a feigned ignorance, return to the tight plausibility structures of farm and village and church.

People who have not experienced this broadening of horizons have never really left the world that they can still regard as natural and the way things are. They have not truly experienced pluralism as something that affects them or their view of the world. For those still dwelling in traditional societies, what is different still appears as odd and strange, not—as it does to the intellectual—as a new wrinkle on a familiar theme. But once out in the wider world, once the basic comparisons have been made between *us* and *them* from the standpoint not of competition but of analysis, it becomes impossible to *be* any longer either us or them—the distance from both is equally great.

The plight of the deracinated intellectual is not restricted to individuals. The world is increasingly divided between those who have been initiated into societal skepticism and those who have not. The more pronounced this division, the greater are the tensions between the two groups. Those who enjoy a rich sense of belonging and a shared view of the world also tend toward intolerance, suspicion, and stultification. Those who have grown into an awareness of the larger world find enlightenment thin gruel for the living of a life, and ironic detachment small comfort during a life of long loneliness. So great is the terror of normlessness, in fact, that the most intellectually liberated often find themselves ready captives for ideological fixes, committing themselves uncritically to programs for a better world, believers not in God but in a variety of utopias.

The social dimension of human life also enables freedom as much as it constrains it. This aspect of society is important for the proper understanding of the life of the Spirit. People do not simply relate themselves as individuals to society as such or as a whole. Society in that sense is as abstract a noun as God. Rather, people encounter every day their parents and spouses, lovers and friends and children, and strangers on the bus. Their social world is filled not with abstract roles but very specific people, with whom they enter into a rich variety of combinations and conflicts.

We are not eyeless monads, objects careening through a world filled only with other objects. Nor are we solitary subjects gazing at the universe. We know and love, ignore and hate, envy and admire other subjects like ourselves, who in turn know and love, ignore and hate, envy or admire us. And as we are both blessed and cursed with spirit, so that our freedom must form a project of becoming a person, so also are all these other subjects each involved in the same process, although—and this is a critical point—their project may look quite different than ours.

Our bodies join in passion, bump into each other when reaching at the same moment for the same hammer, make way for each other in line. Our emotions wash against each other in fear and desire, anger and laughter. Most importantly, we can look not only into each others' eyes but also into each others' minds and hearts in knowledge and love. Our spirits touch in teaching and learning, in speaking and listening. We become enemies, and more remarkably, friends. We make contracts and covenants. We wage war and make peace. We live in a world of other subjects whom we can greet as "thou" as we recognize that they are an "I."

The intersubjective dimension of our existence is of such critical importance because it means each individual's project of freedom inevitably encounters other such projects, other freedoms, other subjects. Each person's project is thereby placed in a situation of possible competition or cooperation. Since it is impossible for two bodies to occupy the exact same spot, it is also impossible for two perceptions to be totally identical. It is therefore impossible as well for two freedoms to be automatically in agreement on a decision. Hence, the drama: will I make my project absolute and override any other perspective? Will I deny my project in favor of that presented by another? Will I grow into another's viewpoint by relativizing my own? Will I similarly invite another to grow by sharing my project and perspective? Will we together form a shared project, and thereby a community?

The Interpretive Dimension

The final dimension of human freedom requiring discussion is what scholars would call its hermeneutical aspect. In simpler terms, we are creatures who seek meaning, and are compelled to interpret our lives. Where our freedom finds its center, in fact, depends a great deal on what meaning we assign to our lives. Our project of becoming a person shapes and is shaped by our interpretation of the world.

I am not speaking here about theoretical explanations of the world, but the stories we tell ourselves and each other. These stories, much more than scientific theories, have a great deal to do with the way we think and feel and act. Anthropologists call such stories myths, not because they are untrue, but because they account for such major matters as human origins, destiny, and obligations with the weight of ultimate authority. Each of us carries around in his or her head a complex set of such stories.

Some myths are provided by the larger culture: This is how we understand the origins and purpose of humanity. Some are told by the political order: Here is what it means to be a successful citizen. Some are supplied by various subgroups in which we have membership: Here is the standard of the good lawyer. Some are given us by the family: This is the norm for being a good wife or a loving child. The narratives do not always agree. To some extent, the story each of us tells about himself or herself draws in idiosyncratic ways from this network of narratives, to construct a story of who I am and what I am about. There is already something of freedom in this, for I can allow myself to be completely defined by these stories external to myself (either in combination or by selecting among them), or I can revise them in the light of my own experience of reality.

The possibility of such revision is given by the dialectic between experience and myth that structures human consciousness. My story (or our myth, if we are speaking of a group) does not only interpret my experience after it happens, in the sense of explaining it. Its prior and more important function is in *shaping* my experience. In our culture, we "see" the sun setting in the west, and see lightning flash; in another symbolic universe we might see the sunset as the dying of our god, or the lightning as signals from alien spaceships.

Our perception is constitutive of our experience, not by certifying what takes place out there, but by affecting what takes place in here. A classic example is provided by the warrior and the ethnographer at the same war dance. They obviously experience something quite different because of their perceptions. In one case, the stance of observer enables some responses and blocks others. In the other case the role of participant and believer blocks a view of the whole, but enables the experience of transforming energy.

In the ordinary way of things, our experiences confirm our myths and, by so doing, strengthen our previous perception of the world. Our understanding that a smile and handshake signal friendliness is confirmed every time these gestures are repeated. But our experiences can also threaten our understanding. When a friend seizes my hand not in friendship but in violence, my symbolic world is threatened. Likewise, when an enemy bandages my wounds with tenderness, my mythic structure is challenged. Such is the shock of hearing cultured speech from a street person, or the glimpse of murderous rage in a physician.

Sometimes, indeed, experience can be sufficiently radical and powerful to shatter our myths. It is impossible to maintain the domestic myth of a happy family when a son has killed his parents in a rage. It is impossible to maintain the myth of an enlightened Europe in the face of two World Wars and the Holocaust. It is extraordinarily difficult to maintain the private story that I am in control when I am in the chaos of narcotic addiction.

Such powerfully disconfirming experiences create for individuals or cultures what sociologists call a state of cognitive dissonance. The term describes a fundamental tension between one's view of the world and one's experience. And because we are creatures who must find meaning, we cannot endure such tension for too long a time. We want to resolve the dissonance. Even here, we have some freedom. We can deny the experience and flee to our previous understanding of things. The cost of this resolution is obvious: we close ourselves to any new experience. Conversely, we can acknowledge the experience and abandon our previous understanding of the world altogether. This is an honest response, but it also has a cost: we are like amnesiacs who don't know what to do next because we don't know how the story has run up till now.

Finally, we can resolve cognitive dissonance by reinterpreting our symbols in the light of our experience. This way of resolving the dissonance is arduous and risk-filled, because it means choosing to live within another sort of tension. It means constant revision of our story. We must fumble about with the broken pieces of our myth, trying to make sense of our experience, even while we continue to live, even while new data pours in.

The first two options are closures. If we deny experience in favor of our previous story, we close the door to any further experience, except that which confirms our story; we cannot change or grow. If we deny our previous story in order to acknowledge our experience, we close the door to meaning and to any possibility of continuity in our lives. We can only move randomly from one experience to the next. Our lives no longer make up a story but a series of episodes. Only the last option creates an openness both to new experiences and to new levels of meaning and understanding.

This dialectic of myth and experience does not take place only at the level of the larger culture. We are, each of us, engaged in the process of revisionist history with regard to our personal stories of who we are and what our project in the world is. These personal stories are not defined completely by the experiences of the larger society. They are shaped by our direct experience of the world and our encounter with other persons, each of whom also has a story. The most immediate and ordinary challenge to our private story is posed by our everyday encounters with these other persons. Such encounters force us to choose between competition and cooperation. When we are willing to tell our story to another, we signal trust. When we are willing to listen to another's story, we acknowledge the other as "thou." Likewise, when we refuse to reveal our story, we reject intimacy; when we lie or distort our story, we pervert dialogue; when we close our ears to another's story, we reduce the other to object.

It is not sufficient simply to define humans in terms of spirit and the project of freedom. It is necessary to examine the specific dimensions of this freedom. As we note the physical, psychological, social, and interpretive dimensions of human life, we recognize that each dimension represents both a limitation and an enabling of freedom. Each puts barriers to the random disposition of our self. But each also presents an opportunity to the spirit to exercise freedom, precisely in the stance taken toward those limitations. We see that it is possible to close the project of becoming a person by fixating on physical fulfillment, or psychological health, or the meeting of societal roles, or the rigid maintenance of our myth in the face of experience. It is also possible for humans to incorporate each of these dimensions into their project, yet remain open to the world, free in a still more fundamental sense.

In these first two chapters, I have attempted to sketch what must be said about the players in the drama of the life of the spirit, examining in turn critical concepts about God and about the human project. In each case I have tried to respect the limits of the respective language games. In speaking of God, I used the symbols of the Christian creed and story. In speaking of humanity, I used words as secular as possible. The most important task is to see how these players enter into dialogue, but before we can do that, we need to describe the conditions which enable that dialogue. I turn next to setting that stage.

3

Setting the Stage: Revelation as a Process of Interpretation

I have spoken of the living God as the power that impinges on the world at every moment. I have described the human project as an open-ended process of becoming a person, a project enabled by the freedom of the human spirit. It is now necessary to bring the players of the drama onto the same stage. How do humans encounter God implicitly when they engage the world? How is the project of human freedom related to the power of God?

I will argue that God discloses power and presence implicitly in the processes of the world as we experience it; that God's self-disclosure is never obvious and self-validating, and is always capable of being denied; that some human experiences intimate God's power and presence more than others, but none do so unambiguously; that every such experience is inevitably clothed in the symbols of the one having the experience, and therefore is a matter of inter-pretation, not only after but during the experience itself.

The topic here is revelation. The alert reader may have been surprised that in the first chapter "God as Revealer" was not a critical theological concept. There are good reasons for delaying its consideration until now. First, the conviction that God is Revealer—although never stated as such there, either—is implicit in all the other claims of the creed. If God the Creator is more than first fashioner, is indeed the first cause of all other causes at every moment, then both the capacity to reveal and the fact of revelation are given with the fact of creation, as they are also with the statements that God is Judge, Savior, and Sanctifier.

Another reason to delay talk about revelation is that proper understanding depends on appreciating it as part of the human project of freedom, involving all the physical, psychological and social dimensions discussed in the last chapter, and above all involving the process of interpretation. I am not suggesting something radical or new here, but something thoroughly traditional. Its point, however, has become more poignant in the circumstances of modernity.

If we think of God in terms of Spirit rather than as a physical object out there, then it is obviously nonsense to say that God could ever be perceived "as God is" by humans, whose perceptions are conditioned by the categories of time and space. Pertinent here is an axiom of scholastic philosophy, *quidquid recipitur per modum recipientis recipitur*: "Whatever is received is received according to the capacity of the receiver." The common sense applications of this axiom will receive ready agreement: A blind eye cannot receive light, a dry battery cannot be charged, a bucket cannot contain the ocean. Likewise, a person with perfect pitch can both appreciate and be pained by music in a way inconceivable to someone who is tone deaf. Color blindness inhibits full appreciation of both sunset and painting. The same principle applies as well to the experience of God: Any such experience is inevitably shaped to the capacity of the one experiencing.

Experience and Interpretation

It makes perfectly good sense to conclude from this that some people have a greater capacity for certain kinds of experiences than do others. It follows as well that one person's experience can be denied by another not because the detractor has a greater capacity but less sensitivity of a certain kind. We who have adequate but scarcely absolute pitch find it difficult to grasp that music sounding fine to us could cause another acute pain. A sunset is simply a lovely rumor to one without sight. How much more subject to denial or skepticism are the claims to having experienced visions, miracles, visitors from out there, or the claim to having encountered something more behind the surface phenomena available to others. There will be no experience or claim concerning "God's revelation" that is utterly self-validating.

Another conclusion takes a bit more courage to state directly. If human experiences are fundamentally shaped by human symbols, then identifying what we experience depends on the symbols available to us, and how our consciousness is shaped by those symbols. Three of us in this room may hear a loud boom, see a flash of light, feel fear. I say it is thunder, but you say it is an angel, and our friend says it is a UFO. All of us experience *something*, and experience something real. The nature and significance of the experience are constituted by our interpretation. Every human experience, however powerful, frightening or transforming, is conditioned by human consciousness.

Some experiences are powerful enough in themselves to alter our interpretations, and shatter our myths. For many alive today, the Holocaust was such an experience: some six million Jews were systematically exterminated in Nazi Germany simply because they were Jews. The Holocaust is so awesome a reality that for a time it silenced both perpetrators and participants, and fragmented the symbolic world of Judaism. But even that experience is now—despite the physical evidence and testimony of eyewitnesses on both sides— actually being denied by some. By others, it is relativized in importance, reevaluated, and reinterpreted as other events succeed it.

The element of interpretation can be appreciated by observing a contemporary claim to experience that is far less public than the Second World War. There are many people today who claim to have seen, encountered, and even communicated with visitors from outer space. Such people appear as sober, honest folk. They describe scenes with remarkable consistency. They show burnt patches on the ground. They pass lie detector tests and remain steady under hypnosis. They show others burns on their skin and medical records connecting the scars to the events in question. The witnesses do not appear to be crazy loners, but family members who had incredible experiences while driving home from the movies. Yet, for all their sincerity and evidence, the majority of people in our culture—certainly the majority of educated people—deny the occurrence of such "close encounters." The experiences are explained in a variety of ways. The societal myth—which in this case is the scientific myth—excludes the possibility of such experiences. Or, if not the experiences, the *interpretation* given the experience by those who had it.

Other people in the late 1980s travelled thousands of miles to the small town of Madjegore, Yugoslavia, to participate—as millions before them had sought to participate in places such as Lourdes and Fatima and Guadalupe—in the experience of another sort of alien visitor, this time the Blessed Virgin Mary, said to have appeared regularly to a group of young villagers. The teenagers were tested, prodded, examined, psychoanalyzed, without satisfactorily disconfirming their stories. They seemed themselves to be naively sincere, incapable of perpetuating so consistent a fraud over such a long time under such public gaze. Yet, however many shared in that *event*, no one besides the children had the *experience*. Only they "saw" and "spoke with the lady" and nodded wide-eyed in synchronized prayer.

Do the UFO witnesses and the Madjegore witnesses experience something real? Are they experiencing something different, or the same thing, but shaped differently because of the shape of their consciousness? It is difficult to decide such matters. I bring up these examples to underscore the point that even powerful and public revelatory experiences are open to denial and multiple interpretations. Some people have such experiences, others don't. Some people identify their experience one way, others differently. A great deal seems to hinge on the perceptions made available to this person or that by their symbols. One wonders, in fact, whether there were any experiences of aliens before the symbols for such an experience were made available by science-fiction in the twentieth century, and whether the same sort of physical and psychical events were not experienced by previous generations in terms of heavenly ascent and the visitation of angels.

The term revelation, therefore, properly describes less a divine activity than a process of human interpretation. In one sense, this conclusion places us in a position of relativism. It is impossible to prove the validity of any interpretation to everybody, or even the reality of an experience to those not willing to enter into our interpretation. But the relativism is not total. In the first place, we might observe that symbols can be more or less adequate to *receive* certain experiences; a consciousness conditioned by symbols of transcendence is capable of experiencing the world in a way impossible to a consciousness completely devoid of such symbols. The symbol, angel, in other words, *enables* perceptions that the symbol, thunder, does not.

In the second place, a given society may structure a group consciousness—both through its structuring of the world and its explanations of the world—in a way that enables or forecloses certain kinds of experiences. If I inhabit a world in which my only contact with water is through pipes and faucets, and never see or hear or swim in the ocean, I think of water in a very different way than the person who sails in deep waters. If my symbolic world is entirely one of physical processes, a closed and mechanistic system of cause and effect, a universe of natural laws that define and determine all possibilities, so that I can speak no longer of the soul or even of the mind but only of the brain, so that I cannot speak of altruism or love but only of sublimated self-interest or sexual drives, then I simply *cannot* experience the world as open, giving, revealing mysteries. My symbols cannot bear such freight. Certain experiences are excluded by an explanatory system that flattens all reality to a single set of factors.

Such is the world most of us in the developed, industrialized, technocratic West inhabit. It is the world of the Enlightenment, of modernity, amplified and refined by the theories of Darwinism, Freudianism, Marxism; a world that not only denies the possibility of God's existence and claim on the world, but has structured societal consciousness in such fashion that the denial appears ever more plausible. In such a world, speaking of transcendence appears odd, even crazy, for the society is structured on (and has a stake in) the effective denial of transcendence. That this is the case is shown by my need to write this chapter. It no longer makes self-evident sense to any one of us to say that God speaks. We must defy the dominant symbols of our world in order to assert that possibility. We are conditioned by the worldview of modernity (our worldview) to think that language about God has no real reference in reality but only expresses subjective states of mind or emotion.

An alternative symbolic system is offered us by our tradition, which speaks of a God who creates anew at every moment and who presses on us in our encounters with the world. This worldview opens our consciousness (however obliquely) to the experience and perception of God in the world. It *enables* revelation by providing the symbols necessary for revelation. By providing this optional view of the world, the creed also gives us the freedom—perilous to be sure—to choose another construal of the world and another interpretation of our (always ambiguous) experience, than that of the dominant culture. What validates this construal of experience as one open to God and involving God? Only the experience of the world it enables, only the project of human freedom it engenders, only the sort of self it yields, only the finished human called the saint, only the ordering of human existence called the rule of God.

If God is the Ultimate Power who creates the world anew at every moment and thereby can be encountered implicitly in the project of human freedom; and if what we call Revelation is the human process of interpretation that goes on both before, during, and after such encounters, then we must assert that revelation is itself a never-ending, open-ended process. If God is a living God whose action always precedes us, then the experience of God in the world is also ever renewed; and so is the interpretation of God. The data continues to come in, the subject matter of theology never stands still, for the subject is the encounter between the living God and the project of human freedom. The potential for revelation, in short, is given by every leaf and stone, every day's living, every human encounter; whether revelation takes place depends on the construal of the event by human freedom.

The attentive reader will by now have noticed that I have been alternating between two kinds of languages. For a time, I use the language of human philosophy and social sciences. Using this language, I am full of caution and constraint; certainty is something to be hinted at rather than asserted. But then I shift to the language of the Christian creed, and when I do, I am full of positive affirmation: God is a living Power; revelation is open-ended. This alternating linguistic usage is purposeful. It is, in fact, demanded by the peculiar choice of being Christian while living in a world fashioned by modernity. The truth of our condition must be approached dialectically. We assert the determinism of the social sciences but then also deny them. We affirm the freedom of the human spirit but also qualify it. In this back and forth movement, this oscillation, we find not only the proper activity of our minds in a world at once manifestly closed and yet intriguingly open; we find as well the paradigm for the path of Christian spirituality as a never-ending oscillation between idolatry and faith. More on that later.

Before examining the human response to God, we need to consider more thoroughly the issue of God's availability. In defining revelation, I asserted *that* God encounters us. But can we say anything more about *how* God encounters us, or say it in a way that respects what we have established about the inevitable constraints imposed by human consciousness and symbolic structuring? I think that we can, by way of analogy and metaphor.

Religious Experience

Rather than debate the theoretical possibilities of encountering God, we may make more progress by considering the accounts of those who claim to have had such encounters and the analysis of such experiences found in the phenomenology of religion. The data comes from every culture in every age. It is contained in the reports of eyewitnesses concerning dreams and visions and unexpected meetings, in the tales of folklore and legend, in the myths of tribes, the scriptures of diverse people. When these accounts are studied comparatively, they reveal remarkably consistent traits, which enable us to speak in broad, typical terms of religious experience and of the structuring of life that is centered around such experience.

In diverse ways, such accounts speak of an encounter with a power that is utterly "Other," off the scale of normal expectations. Wherever encountered—in weird cave or charismatic speaker, in starry desert night or burning bush—the Other is active and challenging. Its power is not always experienced as personal or even as positive. But the encounter has an urgent force that places the human subject in question, demanding an adequate response to its intrusion. Descriptions of such experiences emphasize their suddenness and unexpectedness, their inexplicable occurrence. They are not, say the sources, experiences generated by prayer or magical formula or drugs. Instead, the powerful Other breaks the plane of everyday life, shatters the veneer of predictability, and challenges the presumption of human control.

Analysis of the experience isolates a distinct sort of stimulus and a typical sort of response. The stimulus is uniformly regarded as ultimate power, no matter what the occasion or location of its intrusion. The mountain or tree or cave is not the point, but the power that radiates through such things. The response involves the whole person. It is not merely a matter of the mind or of the will, an idea about ultimacy or a decision to act in a certain way. But neither is it simply a matter of bodily encounter and emotional response. The whole person responds with a peculiar intensity that identifies this as a *sui generis* experience.

The human response to such manifestations of power is best characterized as acute attentiveness. If the "totally Other" appears as raw power, uncontrollable and incomprehensible, the human subject is caught between fear and attraction. In the encounter itself, the human subject is reduced to a state of contingency, powerlessness. The most immediate and understandable impulse is to flee. At the same time, however, this urgent force is magnetic, drawing the human subject to itself. The human is attracted by a life greater than her own.

To this point, the description of religious experience would be difficult to distinguish from aesthetic experience. Certainly the sight of a sunset or the hearing of great music can transport us, place us in contact with a certain sort of ultimacy, make us aware of our own paltriness, and involve all of our capacities of knowing and feeling in profound engagement. But aesthetic experiences, no matter how powerful, are self-sufficient, self-contained. The truly distinguishing feature of religious experience is its element of *command*: the way it demands a restructuring of life around itself.

When religious experiences are sufficiently powerful, they can structure entire societies. Time and space alike are differentiated, on the basis of a central experience of transforming power, into the realms of the sacred and the profane. Sacred time is the time of beginnings, or fresh power; the further one moves away from that point, the less powerful time feels. The task of myth is to return us to the experience of power that established us in the world. Sacred space is defined by the appearance of power in the world. Not only do we build temples and shrines, places for the performance of ritual to define and control the place of power; we organize other space, indeed all of life, around what is seen as most powerful.

A shared religious experience also creates a fellowship of participants around itself. This community perpetuates itself through myth and ritual, but also by its tradition. The founding experience is thus communicated to succeeding generations, not only in the form of the stories recounting the experience, but also in the form of doctrine, which abstracts from myth its enduring principles concerning the proper interpretation of the world. The community also formulates a moral code appropriate to the founding experience. The line between the sacred and the profane is extended by these less power-laden but significant articulations of religious experience.

The best evidence for the fact and force of religious experience, therefore, is the existence of *religion* as an inclusive structuring of life. Not only in the great world religions but equally in tribal cults; not only in canonical scriptures but equally in living oral traditions; not only in stories but equally in the demarcation of space and the arrangement of time, is the evidence given for such powerful experiences. But even outside the bounds of recognized religious fellowships and symbolization, claims to such kind of experiences are made—as in the case of the UFO witnesses—not by people whose behavior marks them as psychotic but by people whose lives are as prosaic as their speech.

Evaluations.   What stance should we adopt toward this mass of data? The simplest response is to reject all such claims as fraudulent, or reduce them to something more manageable. This is the instinctive move of the social sciences: the only thing we can be certain of is that a participant's version of what is happening cannot be accurate. We locate claims about such experiences among undeveloped peoples. Or we attach such perceptions to an unscientific perception of the world. Perhaps "something" happened, but the cause must be other than what the witness thinks. The UFO is really only a meteorite, or satellite, or summer lightning, or the glow from high voltage wires. Forget the scars and burns and haunted eyes of the witnesses, or attribute them to psychosomatic reactions to . . . what? The debunking or reductionistic response is particularly unfortunate, precisely because it is so unscientific. It tends to be both nonempirical and aprioristic.

Dismissal or derogation work so long as they are applied to scattered reports from long ago and far away. They grow increasingly inadequate as responses to stories reported even today in our technological society, not only by the marginalized but even by those whose own scientific credentials are impeccable. The constant need to explain away such phenomena before even attempting to understand them begins to look suspiciously like a form of bad faith.

A totally uncritical acceptance of all such claims at their face value is equally worthless. Some religious claims are undoubtedly fraudulent; "religious" experiences have been used throughout history to gull the credulous and superstitious. Even when the witnesses are sincere, they have only a limited ability to interpret or communicate their experience. We may be open to the fact that *something* happened to them which was real and powerful and important; but we cannot assume that they necessarily understand *what* happened to them.

In any case, since every encounter with the "totally Other" must, by the nature of things, be mediated through what is not totally other—the specific physical and social structures of a particular person or community, as well as the symbols for transcendence available to those who have the experience—we are always in the position of studying the *effects* of such experiences rather than the *causes*, and these effects have a bewildering variety of specific forms. To take the human experience of UFO witnesses seriously, we need not agree about the physical presence of metal spaceships or the physiognomy of the alien visitors. To take seriously the human experience of the witnesses at Madjegore, we need not agree that the Blessed Virgin Mary is physically present and dressed in certain clothes. To take seriously the human experience of the Muslim we need not agree that the Qur'an was dictated in Arabic by the angel Gabriel.

Certain experiences, however, demand to be taken more seriously precisely because they have succeeded in organizing so much time and space. The claim of a tribesman that a certain totem reveals the divine power is fairly easy to dismiss; in fact it is the nature of totems to have power only in a circumscribed space. But the claims made for a Buddha are far more impressive and command a greater attention. The experience in this case is not restricted to a single place or time or even a single human life, but extends to the organization of the lives of millions of human lives all across the world and through many centuries. The inclusiveness and pervasiveness of the *effect* in this case suggests something significant about the profundity and ultimacy of the *cause*.

But to try adjudicating such experiences—determining which is authentically religious and which is not, or worse, which is "from God" and which is not—is a fool's game, precisely because no human being is in a position to make such judgments. If I should tell you that I have had a significant dream that reveals the meaning of my life to me, you may want to attribute the dream either to the beans I ate last night, or to an angel. Neither explanation of cause can be proven or disproven. Nor need they be mutually exclusive. More important, neither explanation of causes helps me understand the meaning of the dream for my life.

A third option for assessing accounts of religious experience is the one I adopt here. On the one hand, I take seriously the reality of the sacred as a fact of human consciousness and as a factor in the structuring of human life. On the other hand, I take equally

seriously the impossibility of getting beyond the sacred as a phenomenon of human consciousness and social structuring to a direct
apprehension of "the Holy" as objective reality. Given my careful
qualifications concerning the interpretation of experience in chapter
two of this book, the reader will not be surprised at this position.
I do not think there is any religious experience that is self-validating
or obviously from God, in the sense that any fair-minded observer
must agree with the witness's account. Yet, if we are to suppose
that God does communicate with humans, then (I affirm with equal
firmness) it must be through such experiences shaped by human
consciousness and social structuring.

Once we are free of the obligation either to defend or disprove
such narratives of religious experience, we are able to appropriate
the extraordinarily helpful categories they provide us for the analysis
of human behavior. We are able to move beyond a preoccupation
with whether this or that experience is really from God to a diagnosis
of human activity as centering in power.

Applications.   When we begin to think of the Holy in functional
terms as that which exercises organizing power over time and space,
the phenomenological analysis of religious experience has many
applications. The deeper dimensions of many ordinary human experiences are thus made accessible. The sacred and the profane do
not appear as two totally separated realms, but as two points in a
continuum of analogous experiences of power.

Nothing can make the applicability of these categories to real life
more evident than the straightforward observation of what for many
people is the most ordinary yet important event in their lives, falling
in love. Picture the normal late adolescent college male, going
through the dreary, profane activities of a semester. He writes papers,
gets homesick, drags through classes. Life is empty, repetitious,
boring. Then, on a trip to the library for a research paper (perhaps
his first such trip all semester), he spots in the stacks the girl of his
dreams. Never has he been so attracted, yet never so afraid. He is
riveted. He wants to meet her, but dares not risk himself with so
glorious a creature. He feels his own inadequacy. At the same time,
her presence fills him with a heightened sense of himself. Let us
suppose he does not approach her, indeed only catches a first
glimpse. She turns the corner of the stacks and disappears.

The young man has had an experience of power. Its significance
is found, however, not only in the way it made him feel at that

moment, but in the way it organizes the rest of his life. He wants
to *participate* in this power that at once frightens and energizes him.
To gain that participation, he rearranges his life in terms of time
and space, even if he is not consciously aware of it. Now, he haunts
the part of the library where he had seen the girl (third floor stacks),
whereas before he had never visited it. Why? So that he may see
her there again, experience the power again. He arranges his day
so that he can be at that spot at that time every day, hoping to
bump into her again.

When he is in the space where the power appeared, he has a
heightened sense of being. He is at once defined by a power other
than himself, and yet knows that he never has been so truly himself
as when connected to her power. The moment he sees her again,
and, blessedly, talks to her, time itself takes on a new weight. The
rest of his day is only chronology. Every other place is desert. Where
she is (however musty the books) is oasis, is paradise. The power
of new love to structure the patterns of one's life have been celebrated
in song: "You walk down the street on the chance that you meet,
and you meet, not really by chance."

They meet, let us say, tell each other their stories, and join together
in commitment. The power of that first encounter is made more
evident by the continued structuring of their lives together. They
form a fellowship on the basis of that experience. As their lives
continue, and as time works its inevitable erosion of passion, they
can become enlivened again by a retelling of the story in myth and
by the ritual enactment of their commitment in sexual love. The
story is continued in its retelling to children, together with the
lessons of doctrine and morality that can be derived from the tale.

This example is obviously abbreviated and idealized. But the
pertinence of the categories of religious experience should be obvious. There is the encounter with the other; the response of awe;
the sense of contingency and dependence; the moment of revelation
both of the other and the self; the restructuring of life; the formation
of a fellowship with its activities of myth and ritual, doctrine and
morality. And in all of this, the process of becoming a self by being
related to that which is more powerful than oneself.

The story of falling in love is particularly evocative. It is important
to my argument because in that experience, power is located in
another subject, and the encounter is dialogical. It will form one of
the most important of the analogies available to us when we speak
of our response to God. For now I need only note that the same

analysis can be applied to many other appearances of power in the world. The power exercised over a crowd by a charismatic speaker; the dramatic and powerful changes in an adolescent's body because of puberty; the powerful physical emergence into the world of a child, first in the inexorable progression of pregnancy and then in helpless yet remarkably world-structuring birth; the appearance of a cancer; the quiet gift of acceptance by a stranger—all of these bear some of the characteristics of religious experience. Indeed, humans cannot avoid such encounters. They are a corollary of our spirits being embodied in the world.

In this chapter, I have tried to spell out as fully as possible my understanding of revelation, not as a product delivered by God but as a human process of interpreting experience. I have stated emphatically my conviction *that* God is disclosed implicitly in human experience. I have tried by analysis of religious and analogous experiences to describe *how* such disclosure can take place. By locating this process in the human encounter with otherness in the world, I am able to affirm at once its reality—it happens all the time— and its open-ended, tentative nature.

It is appropriate now to repeat the most fundamental conviction of the Christian creed: God is Creator of heaven and earth. As I define this, it means that God impinges on the world and creates it new at every moment. Wherever humans encounter the power of an *other*, (any other), therefore, an encounter with *the* Other who is God is implicitly present as well. This means, at the least, that the way we respond to all the "others" in the world is, in fact, also the way we respond to the unseen God. And since such encounters are unavoidable and constant—even when we separate ourselves from other people, we can not avoid altogether the otherness of our own bodies and the physical world—both the process of revelation and the process of its acceptance or rejection takes place throughout every human lifetime, never ceasing before death. And, since the process takes place within the project of each human being, every human narrative is potentially (if it can be made articulate) a narrative of idolatry and sin, of grace and faith. To that most basic drama of all, I now turn.

4

The Basic Drama:
Idolatry, Sin, Grace, Faith

*T*he path to Christian maturity leads from slavery to freedom. Progress along that path is, however, seldom direct and never certain. In this chapter, I sketch the drama that is the human project of life before God. In its essentials, the drama is simple, consisting in four basic elements: idolatry, grace, sin, and faith. A preliminary plot outline can provide a framework for the later discussion of these components in the complexity of their interactions.

Everything discussed in the earlier chapters should be carried forward by the reader: the definition of the human project both in terms of freedom and of multiple conditioning; the conviction that God's power and presence is implicit in the world that God creates at every moment; the analysis of the encounter between the human subject and the Other within the structures of this world in terms of the patterns established by power. I attempt now to pull these separate analyses into a single dynamic process of interaction between God and humans. I will suggest that the natural tendency of human freedom is toward idolatry; that freedom from idolatry is enabled by God's offer of grace; that sin is the refusal and faith is the acceptance of that gift.

Each of these terms is rooted in Scripture and in Christian tradition. Because they are so central to Christian symbolism, they have been both heavily used and variously understood. Part of my present task is to define these concepts in a way that is consonant with their biblical roots and theological traditions, and above all in a way that corresponds to the real experience of the world.

Idolatry

When we read attacks on idolatry in the ancient prophets, we may miss their real significance. They make idolatry sound almost quaint, and the polemics look like a competition between rival deities, with the Israelite prophets claiming: "Our God is greater than your God." Perhaps that is even what they meant when first composed. All the Scripture, however, has the ability to point beyond its first historical circumstances to perennial issues of the human condition. Read this way, the attacks on idolatry describe a real difference between perceptions of the world and therefore a real difference in manner of life.

Idolatry means treating what is not ultimate as though it were ultimate, making absolute what is only relative. Idolatry is a meaningful concept only within the framework of radical monotheism. If we believe that there is only one ultimate Power from whom all things derive and toward which all things are ordered, not as independent entities but as creatures, then the service of any creature as ultimate must be regarded as deception and distortion.

The Bible's most extensive attacks on idolatry are found in The Wisdom of Solomon 13–15 and Rom. 1:18-32. They properly define idolatry not as a competition between cults, but as a disease of the human spirit. It is a disease so pervasive that it persuasively counterfeits health. Wisdom and Paul describe idolatry in its social as well as its individual dimensions. Taking the lead from them, we can call idolatry the Big Lie about reality. It is spoken in the heart of the individual person, but it is echoed and reinforced by society's systemic distortions of the truth.

The Natural Perversion.   We begin our analysis of the spiritual life with idolatry, because that is where the life of our human spirit begins. Idolatry comes naturally to us, not only because of the societal symbols and structures we ingest from birth, but also because it is the easiest way for our freedom to dispose itself. On the evidence, our freedom seems to like nothing so much as slavery.

The roots of idolatry lie deep within the human heart, in the terror generated by the awareness that we are empty, powerless, dependent, contingent beings. The indeterminacy of our spirit, which we described in the previous chapter, does not strike us as a benefit but as something truly frightening. If we do not have a "being" given to us as a finished product, we also do not have an automatic sense of worth, of "necessity." If our self is not given to us by nature, we must construct it. And if our worth does not consist in what we are, we must gather it from what we have. Idolatry therefore seeks something powerful enough to give us being, life, and worth, yet controllable enough so that it will be *our* being, life, and worth.

Here the essential human instinct of centering comes into play. Since we have no center given us by nature we must, it appears, make or find a center sufficiently strong to sustain us. Our freedom fixes on something that can make us a self. All of this seems perfectly natural. Where does the lie come in? It comes first in the denial of the one ultimate power that holds me in existence at every moment; it appears second in the pretension that anything created by that one power could replace it as a source of life and worth. Because everything but the One God is derivative and dependent, nothing created can serve as sufficient source for what the human spirit seeks.

The prophets parodied the arduous efforts expended by idolaters in propping up their statues of wood and stone. These idols, said the prophets, had no life or power of their own, and had to depend on the power of their worshipers to exist. There is both grim humor and deep truth in that charge. When the spirit—which is potentially open to all things—seeks a self in any created thing, makes that thing ultimate and the source of life and meaning, then the human spirit becomes enslaved. The objects of our worship require our constant attention if they are to remain gods, because they have no necessity of their own. The essential sign of the idolatrous spirit, therefore, is *compulsion*, which is simply a clinical term for enslavement. I must maintain this project, for it will collapse if I do not. Yet this is the project I pretend gives *me* my life! Idolatry begins in fear and ends in compulsion.

Idolatry perverts the truth of reality in three interconnected ways. It lies first about the self. No finite thing *can* provide life and worth to the human spirit. When human freedom fixates on any such limited thing as absolute, the self shrivels and shrinks to the level of the object worshiped. The project that promised freedom becomes a form of slavery, for it can be maintained only by unceasing effort.

Second, idolatry also perverts our relationship with other creatures. If we single out some finite aspect of the world and treat it as absolute, fixing our freedom on its service, we prevent as well the true use of other things. All our attention goes to what we serve, leaving us no room for anything else. Third, idolatry distorts the very thing we worship. No finite thing can bear the burden of being divine. By being made absolute, created things become grotesque caricatures of themselves.

The Varieties of Idolatry.   The idolatrous impulse can express itself variously, although the basic options are drearily predictable. We can fix our freedom on just about anything, can serve anything as the be-all and end-all of our existence, the source of our hope and our worth. Some of us stop with the body. We can center our existence around the avoidance of pain and the pursuit of delight. We can cater to one appetite more than another, although not surprisingly they tend to cancel each other. Total attention given to gastronomic delight deflects or disables interest in sexual pleasure. Conversely, complete satyriasis renders a man skinny. We can also fixate on the body's appearance as an absolute good, enduring a wearying regimen of observance: diet, exercise, ointments, face-lifts, muscle-toning, stylish dress, fastidious makeup. Such hard work tends to cancel catering to pleasure. Equally obsessive-compulsive behavior is demanded if the body's survival or health is made an ultimate goal: what careful attendance on caloric intake, on proper peristalsis, on cardio-vascular efficiency! I walk, but not too fast; I jog, but with a finger monitoring my heart-beat. What avoidance of dangerous elements: poisons, carcinogenics, toxic wastes, viruses, unhealthy people!

How fragile must be the sense of being and of worth, when located entirely in the body! How frantically must we maintain our efforts: holding back aging, avoiding sickness. How isolated must we become, for other people are more a threat than a blessing: they are useful as they stimulate my appetites, or admire and crave my beauty, or help me preserve my life. But they are also competitors for pleasure, beauty, survival.

A similar rigidity is required of us if we make the state of our souls the ultimate good. If we identify our being and worth with emotional equanimity, we must defend ourselves against whatever might threaten that stability. We cannot afford to feel certain emotions or to put ourselves in a situation where they might be evoked.

Again, the other that confronts or challenges that emotional equilibrium must be repelled. The same pattern is found when moral virtue is made an absolute project. We must exercise constant vigilance over the purity of our own motives, the excellence of our virtue, the nobility of our character, the consistency of our behavior. Compulsion is more subtle when serenity or sanctity is the project, but is no less enslaving.

Idolatry is a disease that infects society as well as the individual, and when it becomes systemic idolatry is more difficult to escape. Humans accept as natural and necessary the values of the group into which they are socialized. They accept society's judgment concerning life and worth: what is important, what counts as success. The tendency of human freedom to fixate on a power it can control as the source of its identity is exacerbated by a society that indoctrinates its members to think that youth, health, beauty, wealth, and strength are the goals of life and the source of worth.

Society can also have its own distinctive idolatries that reveal the same patterns of fear and compulsion. A nation may have as its express ideals the freedom, peace, and prosperity of its citizens. But if it absolutizes its own survival as the sole means to provide these benefits, the nation can perceive other nations as threats to its own survival, and therefore (it is rationalized) to these values for which we stand. The fear of annihilation leads it to ever greater defensive efforts; the "preservation of liberty" remains the rationale, but now less convincingly. The more rigidly the defenses are maintained, the more the values they were intended to serve become eclipsed. We see a nation dedicated to life and freedom engaging in oppression and murder—not alone of alien peoples, but even of its own people. In the name of liberty, the nation's own citizens can find themselves subject to spying, suspicion, social control, impoverishment, and even violence—not from foreign enemies, but from the assigned protectors of their freedom.

The concept of idolatry applies to society in still another way. Social institutions by their very nature tend to make themselves absolute, and demand idolatrous service from their members. Social institutions are inherently fragile, because they are creations of human consensus. People must pretend that a certain social form is necessary and natural for it to continue in existence at all. Institutions therefore tend to demand all the life from their members, for they *need* all that life to make plausible their claim to be real. Social structures have no built-in capacity to relativize themselves.

An example of an idolatrous social institution is religion itself. Our previous discussion here comes to a tight focus. Idolatry is itself a religious concept. And we have seen in our analysis of "religious experience" in chapter three how humans center themselves, organize their existence, around sources of power which they experience as ultimate. It is a natural tendency for the individual person to identify the power that is experienced with the symbol of its expression. Thus, I can reduce and control the mysterious other, whose power I cannot control, by focusing on the medium of its expression, which I can control. Temples, shrines, feasts, rituals, sacrifices, creeds, codes: all mediate the experience of power. How easy to fixate on the means rather than on the source!

When we join in a religious fellowship—a social institution created by such an experience of power—how easy it is, how natural, given the inertia of all social institutions, for religion to claim an absoluteness and ultimacy for *itself* rather than for the power it first mediated. How simple—and what a pleasure for humans who in any case are looking for as quick a closure to their freedom as they can find—to serve with compulsive and rigid devotion this symbol of the Holy rather than The Holy One. No more than any other social institution does religion as such have the capacity to relativize itself.

We can speak of idolatry in functional terms as the centering of human life around some perceived power. We thereby are provided with a diagnostic tool of the first importance for the life of the Spirit. Idolatry in this sense is not an abstract set of erroneous opinions, but the most concrete structuring of human life. We can move—carefully to be sure—by means of analysis from the *patterns* of behavior to the *power* which structures them. And since idolatry is essentially a form of compulsion protecting us against existential fear, we can also move analytically from the deployment of our defenses to the points of our greatest vulnerability.

Much of our life, of course, is spent in the upkeep and maintenance of structures that we have not ourselves created; but even within the constraints of social role and occupation, we each structure our lives to possess what we regard as most powerful and important, or conversely, to avoid what we most fear. Observe the way we organize the time and space available to us. The pattern reveals what is ultimate for us, our functional god.

The addict is the best example, because addiction makes most explicit what applies implicitly to everyone's life. The addict's day is structured around getting and concealing a fix. Time is measured not by the chronology of external events, but by degrees of internal high or withdrawal. Space is structured around places to buy and use the drug; the daily round is defined by purchase and use. What applies to the person addicted to drugs applies as well in cases of addiction to alcohol, food, sex, work, and applause. The patterns of behavior point toward a centering power.

Less dramatic but no less important are the clues given by our emotions. We ask what elates us or what deflates us; what experiences leave us exultant and what leave us depressed? What feelings do we avoid and what do we encourage? Our emotions provide us another way of assessing the patterns that structure our lives. Our assessments of value also point us to these structuring patterns: Why do I regard some things more highly than others? How do I measure my own success and failure? On what basis do I esteem or condemn others?

The criteria of behavior, emotions, and attitudes tend to coincide. Together, they indicate the place of power around which we center our life and sense of worth. I can lie in bed, sleepless and anxious on a late summer night, and think back through my day. What was the high point and what the low? What made it a good day or bad? What threat or challenge or lack has brought me this vague but real anxiety? The analysis of one day might reveal only a small piece of the overall pattern; but the analysis of weeks and months and years reveals the larger patterns that constitute our personal form of idolatry.

It may appear that I have not exempted any human activity from the charge of idolatry. This is exactly my point. Nothing is more natural to humans than idolatry. There is good reason for our existential fear and for the compulsiveness it generates. There is no human project that we cannot or will not make absolute and ultimate. The differences are a matter of degree: how profound or trivial is the thing we have made ultimate? A person or group totally defined by bodily pleasure or survival is manifestly idolatrous in a more primitive sense than a person or group totally defined by virtue or truth or beauty. An idolatrous system may be more or less adequate for life, include more or less capacity for growth. It can be tested on the basis of what activities it must forbid, and what activities it enables; how much of what is properly human does it truncate and how much does it nurture?

By ourselves, we can never transcend the slavery of the idolatrous impulse. By ourselves, we can never be rid of the primitive fear of non-being and worthlessness, never rid of the need therefore to construct on some palpable basis a worth to which we can point and say, "I have, therefore, I am." Idolatry remains the easiest, most accessible, most societally reinforced closure of our freedom.

I have repeated the phrase, "by ourselves," because in the perspective of Christian faith, it expresses the fundamental lie about humans: that we are by ourselves or on our own, in the world. We can call it a lie, of course, only from the perspective that states as its most fundamental truth that the world comes from a God who is the first and ultimate power, and who creates each of us at every moment, so that, even if we think otherwise, even if our enlightenment myth insists otherwise, we are none of us ever by ourselves, are none of us ever on our own, but are at every moment of our lives intrinsically related to the One who transcends our control and who presses on us in our encounters with the world. This conviction—that there is another actor in the drama more important and powerful than us, who always speaks first—is expressed in the Christian symbol of *grace*. For the human project of becoming a person, grace is the opening to freedom.

Grace

Speaking about grace is difficult for several reasons. We can easily be led by the noun "grace" to treat the reality as though it were a thing. The same thing happens here as with the term revelation. The word is supposed to refer to a dynamic process, but our minds prefer static products. God's grace therefore becomes a package delivered to us—we are assured—during our lives. But since we really have no very specific idea of what "grace" might look like, it is difficult to take the suggested delivery seriously. And a gift unknown is a gift not fully received.

A second problem in talking about grace is that it is a concept that has been hotly debated by theologians through the centuries. Nothing is more likely to render a term useless as its being wrung through the wringer of polemic. Because the term grace received greatest attention in disputes about grace and works (in the Pelagian controversy) and grace and freedom (in the Molinist controversy) it appears fearsomely complicated and a matter for specialists. The debates generated a complex lexicon of adjectives that can be applied to grace. They make us think we are refining our understanding. But if we have no real grasp of what grace is in the first place, we are not much helped by calling it saving grace or sanctifying grace or prevenient grace or actual grace. An adjective does not make a noun more real, only more limited.

I will try to develop here a functional understanding of grace as a verb rather than as a noun. I take seriously the statements of Scripture, first that "every good endowment and every perfect gift is from above, coming down from the Father of lights," (James 1:17) and second, that "by grace" you have been saved (Eph. 2:5). But I take equally seriously the conviction that God is Spirit, and that humans are embodied spirits seeking a self in a project of freedom. The functional analysis of grace should therefore correspond to our analysis of idolatry. We seek to understand grace as part of a dynamic pattern of interaction, as an essential element of the human encounter with the world and thereby implicitly with God.

The Gift of Otherness.   In the broadest sense, I define grace as the gift of otherness made available to us by God in the world. It is the fact that there always *is* an other that enables me to break the pattern of idolatry. Idolatry tries to control the world by making it my self-project. The inertia of idolatry is always toward swallowing up the other in a comprehensive pattern of compulsion. Only if there is an other that escapes my project, that remains outside my control, can my idolatry be relativized; only then can I have the chance to change and grow. This way of putting the case may appear novel, but I think it corresponds precisely to the witness of Scripture and to the activity of human consciousness.

We can start with a series of puzzling and provocative statements by Paul. In 1 Cor. 8:1-3, when speaking of eating food that had been offered to idols, he contrasts "knowledge" and "love." He says, "If anyone thinks he has knowledge, he does not yet know as he should know. But if someone loves God, this person is *known by God.*" Again, in 1 Cor. 13:12, Paul contrasts the present human condition to the future: "For up to now, we are seeing through a mirror in a riddle; then we shall see face to face. Up to now, we know only partially; but then *we shall know just as we are also known.*" Finally, in Gal. 4:8-9, Paul again contrasts two states, this time the condition of the Galatians before and after their conversion: "But then, since you did not know God, you enslaved yourselves to beings that were not by nature gods. But now, since you know God, *or better, since you are known by God,* how can you turn back again to those weak and poor rudiments, and desire to serve them again?" What does Paul mean by being "known by God," and how does this pertain to God's grace? Why does Paul emphasize being known by God over knowing God? Perhaps for this simple a reason: knowing God is compatible with the human project of idolatry; being known and loved by God can only come by way of gift, can never be brought under human control.

Understanding grace in terms of knowing and loving is particularly important, because any exchange between God as Spirit and the human spirit must take place within the activities distinctive and proper to spirit. From the side of the Giver, therefore, we must try to imagine the activity of knowing humans as they truly are and accepting them as they are, by the transcendent Spirit who is available equally to all beings at every moment. From the side of the gifted, likewise, we try to imagine how this being known and loved might be received by an embodied and basically idolatrous human spirit.

When we look closely at the primordial fear that generates the compulsions of idolatry, we perceive that it has a great deal to do with the sense that we are *not* known and loved. Only adolescents are allowed to state clearly what all of us have felt, which is why adolescents are so threatening. They say "No one can possibly know me." And, as a corollary but by no means an afterthought, "Even if I were known, I would not be loved." The desire to be known, we understand intuitively, is the desire to be *real,* to be perceived as existing by another subject. The desire to be loved, likewise, is the desire for *acceptance* by another subject, to be considered worthwhile.

Paradoxically, however—and this is our enslavement—what we most desire at one level, we work hardest to prevent at another. To be known as we really are is too threatening, so we struggle to construct a self that appears more real and substantial. To be accepted as we really are seems impossible, so we seek to control the conditions of others' acceptance and love. Thus out of our fear we work up a more and more impressive performance, hoping to win the approval and applause of others.

Even as the audience applauds our act, even as we are admired and imitated, however, our emptiness grows more apparent, for *we* know that they are perceiving and loving a self that is only fictional, that requires maintenance by our constant effort. Yet we cannot let down, cannot relax, and simply be what we are, for we have no self apart from what we have performed or possessed. The more others are persuaded by the reality of this projected self, the more they are seduced by it, the more entrapped we ourselves become by our past performance. Any revelation now of our empty, needy, vulnerable self would not only be disappointment (we think), but the unmasking of a fraud. Thus, the primordial fear grows steadily more realistic: *now* to be known as I am surely would mean to be rejected.

Experience and introspection alike confirm that this compulsive pattern, once in place, cannot reverse itself. Instead, the project of establishing a self by means of possession and performance becomes ever more urgent and ever more rigid. Everything in the world can potentially be swallowed by my self-aggrandizement, for there is no reason ever to stop possessing or performing. I cannot know and love myself, for I am convinced there is nothing to know or love apart from what I have produced. And precisely my mode of being in the world precludes being known and loved by others, because I constantly set the terms of their perceptions and response. Here, as Paul knew, what I most desire is truly what I do not do.

Yet experience (if not our own, that of others) also tells us that this pattern *can* be broken from outside. Sometimes it happens that we encounter an other that we cannot simply make part of our project, that resists reduction to our performance or possession. Most emphatically, we experience this in other persons who resist our efforts at seduction, who maintain their integrity as subjects, who insist on perceiving us from *their* perspective rather than the one we want to force on them by our aggressive self-presentation, who preserve their ability to accept or reject us on the basis of *their* knowledge rather than on the basis of our manipulation of our image or of their feelings. This is truly a gift that opens the possibility of freedom.

The Gift of Love.   The most powerful example of this gift for most of us is the human experience of love. I am thinking now not of "falling in love" (which in itself as I suggested is idolatrous in form) but the mature experience of loving and being loved. Here, I can only report on my own experience—confirmed by the narratives of others. In this case, I am known by another, not on the basis of my self-presentation that I can control, but on the basis of her perception, which is outside my control. My project is to base my esteem and worth on my accomplishments, my brains, my ability to verbalize or to tap dance. These, I have learned, can win me applause and even affection, although the warmth is never quite enough to allow me rest between acts. But she is not impressed by these. "I do not like tap-dancing, lots of talk, smart-alecks, or the production line," she says, "but I know that you are a warm and good person, and I love you."

Several possibilities are established by the encounter with such an insistent other. First, the very offer of the gift empowers me to make a choice that was previously unavailable. I can accept the gift. By so doing, I allow my own project to be relativized. It loses some of its absolute quality and its rigidity. My project, at the least, becomes temporarily enlarged by stretching to include the freedom of an other. In order to accept the gift, furthermore, I am required to acknowledge the other as other—not myself or a part of my project—and accept the validity of the other's perspective and predilection.

Acceptance of the gift also frees me in a more fundamental sense to be a self. So much of my compulsive production and presentation derived from the fear of being known or accepted, and forced me to seduce every other subject and reduce every other to the project of my self. Now, I am freed to be a receiving, vulnerable, gifted self, not an acquiring, dominating, or controlling self. Allowing myself to be known and accepted by another on that person's terms rather than my own enables me as well to be available to further others on their terms. The gift from another is a call to step into a project larger than my own . . . it invites me into a world greater than that of my own construction. Once released from the absolute constraint of self-definition, I can regard others not as objects for me to possess or control, but as subjects to be known and accepted in turn.

It is also possible for me to refuse the gift of knowledge and acceptance from an other. The gift is a challenge and threat to my own project. To accept another's gift on his or her terms means letting go of my project for the moment—which means letting go of my self as I have previously understood and maintained it. It means losing total control over my project. What can be construed as an invitation to a larger life can also be considered a death threat to the only life I have known.

The fact of the gift enables decision but does not determine it. We can go either way. We can accept another's knowledge and acceptance on the basis of their perception rather than our own presentation. Or, we can reject that gift, and prefer our own labor. Before turning to the Christian symbols for these decisions, a few more remarks on the nature of the gift may be helpful.

The Gift of God.   The first and perhaps the most important thing to assert is that, from the perspective of the Christian creed, humans inhabit a grace-drenched world. If God creates at every moment in the sense we have defined, then the gift of otherness is offered every person at every moment. God is the "giver of every good gift" always and everywhere. When we speak of the process of gifting or gracing as a verb, therefore, we are not talking about something exceptional or rare, but a constant process that is a corollary of God's continuing creation. God's knowledge and love of the world is offered at every moment in its very coming to existence; for human consciousness, therefore, there is in *every* other that is encountered the implicit offer of God's knowledge and love—that is, grace.

The second thing that needs emphatic assertion is that the experience of human love as I have described it is not simply a metaphor for God's grace, or even an analogy. It is a *means* of God's grace, indeed one of the most direct and powerful ways in which God touches the human spirit. But God is able to reach us through every created thing, every other that confronts and challenges our idolatrous project. Confronting the wonders and terrors of the natural world can speak a truth to us, enable us to experience being known and perhaps even being accepted in a way that can challenge and relativize our rigid project of constructing our selves on our own terms.

Even the experience of our own body—in its changes, in its resistance to our plans, in its weakness and disease—can challenge our idolatry and enable us to perceive how we can be known and accepted in terms other than those of our performance. God never runs out of gifts, never ceases giving. Because God is always Other to us, and we can never make God our project, can never reduce the Creator to the level of our creation, we have hope. There is always One who resists our idolatrous project, who *can* gift us precisely because God remains always Other to us.

Third, the reader will notice that my interpretation of grace in terms of being known and accepted by the Other depends not only on the critical theological concept of God as Creator but also the conviction that God is Judge, in the sense earlier defined. The symbol *Judge* enables us to state our conviction that the One who presses upon us in the circumstances of our lives and challenges our pretension to independence and self-sufficiency, is a personal Spirit, and not simply a brute force or energy field, One who *can* therefore know and love. It enables us to express as well the conviction that this act of knowing and accepting is utterly fair and impartial—we cannot bribe this observer. God knows and loves all God's creatures from a perspective that we cannot attain much less control. This is itself a freeing realization.

Fourth, a sobering reminder. God may press upon us as Other in *creation*, but what if we systematically eliminate the possibility of encountering that creation as Other, or otherness as creation? Then it is not simply the natural human tendency toward idolatry that needs relativizing, but the idolatrous project of an entire culture. As we saw earlier, a society based on the systematic denial of transcendence will not find it easy to acknowledge any event as grace. And for every individual person within such an idolatrous culture, the possibilities of encountering the other as Other become limited. This is in fact the current state of affairs for those living in the world of modernity, which is essentially shaped by the denial of such encounter.

The problem for those of us living in the contemporary Western world is not simply that the myth of the age dismisses transcendence as a meaningless category, and purveys symbols incapable of bearing any note of genuine otherness. The problem is that our technological capability has created a world of physical and social systems that, in the most concrete sense, eliminate the otherness of creation. Those living in industrialized, computerized lands rarely if ever encounter the world as other, but only a hominized world that is precisely constructed according to human reason and will.

Those whose feet never touch earth, whose fingers never touch grass, whose eyes never see prairies or starry skies, but who live instead in a controlled environment of cement and plastic and circuitry where nothing alien or unplanned can ever occur—or so the pretension until the electricity fails or the nuclear reactor goes haywire or the crops fail or the toxic waste spreads—can convince themselves, indeed are convinced by the society they inhabit, that there is no Other to encounter. Society can eliminate otherness by its coercive power, shaping members into smooth conformity; or by its censoring power, suppressing difference in thought or belief or action; or by its segregating power, placing those who are different or deviant into safe compartments.

But a lie is no less a lie because it is often repeated, stated loudly, or written in stone and software circuits. The person who experiences electricity only by flipping a switch or monitoring a generator may grow confused about power and who controls what. The person who encounters lightning in an open field is not confused. Bouncing a healthy baby on my knee, I can think that my life is simply a series of problems to solve. Staring into the ravaged eyes of my raped daughter, I must know that life is a mystery that must be suffered. Even in our closed-circuit world, God can grace us with otherness and call us to a project larger than our own. And even in this hermetic, homogenized, hominoid world, we can respond with the fundamental choice of denial or acceptance, closure or openness, sin or faith.

Sin

In Rom. 14:23 Paul says, "whatever does not proceed from faith is sin." How can we understand so inclusive a disjunction? We will not get far if we understand faith simply as belief, or sin simply as the breaking of a commandment. For Paul, faith and sin represent the two basic responses of humans to reality. They are the symbols for the two directions freedom can take when confronted by God's gift of otherness in the world.

Sin is the refusal of God's gift. It is a closure. Like all other dispositions of human freedom, sin is never once-for-all, but is incremental, reaching its completion only in death. There is an obvious connection between idolatry and sin. Both seek to establish existence and worth apart from dependence on the Creator. But there is an equally important distinction between them. Idolatry is built in to our human need to be centered in order to function at all, an almost inevitable human tendency. Even in the perspective of faith, the fact that God has created us with this sort of inertia makes idolatry relatively benign.

The Choice of Idolatry.   Sin, in contrast, is the conscious *choice* of idolatry over grace. The choice is only truly possible when the gift is available; now, the closure to otherness becomes deliberate. I am offered the chance to change and grow. I am offered the knowledge and love of another on terms other than that of my own fear and compulsion, and I choose . . . my own terms. I pick my own enslavement rather than the freedom of a larger project. Here, truly, is the "mystery of iniquity." It is easy to understand our idolatry; nothing makes more sense. But when we are *offered* an alternative, and refuse it . . . this is hard to understand.

The nature of sin is conveyed metaphorically in the Gospel of John, which says, "This is the judgement, that the light has come into the world, and men loved darkness rather than light, because their deeds were evil" (John 3:19). An elaboration of the metaphor can help make the distinction between idolatry and sin. We can, let us say, imagine the world as a dark room completely without light. I have lived in it since birth, and although I stumble about in the room and bruise my shins, and fear its cold corners and must rigidly control my movements to defend against danger, the darkness does not seem dark to me, it is simply the world. The concept of light is meaningless to me. It corresponds to nothing in my experience. But equally meaningless is the concept of darkness.

We can also imagine a crack in the roof letting a bright beam of sunshine into the room. The situation in my world is objectively altered. For the first time, I can see my room as it truly is, and because I have seen light, can also "see" darkness *as* darkness and not simply as the way things are. The otherness of light offers the possibility of a new way of understanding the world. It also enables a new pattern of life in this room; I can move about more freely in the spaces of light; I can better assess the shadows; I need not be so fearful and therefore so rigidly compulsive in my movements.

If the light offers me a new freedom, and the opportunity to change, it also enables me for the first time truly to sin. Now I can *consciously* refuse the offer of true sight. I can, despite the evidence of my eyes, *deny* the reality of the light. I can even close my eyes, return to a state of darkness, and continue to live as I have always lived. But now, something has fundamentally changed. I must *close my eyes* to continue as I had; now my enslavement is not simply a result of my environment but a consequence of my freedom. Offered a new vision of truth, I prefer my old truth, and refuse to see that it is now not a truth at all, but a lie. In a word, sin is the choice of idolatry. If idolatry is a chronic disease of the human spirit, then sin is its acute form, and it is deadly.

The mutilating character of sin is shown first in its effect on the sinner. The refusal of truth leads to the distortion of the self. The Bible uses the images of blindness and deafness for such willful rejection of truth: "Hear and hear, but do not understand; see and see, but do not perceive . . . their ears are heavy of hearing and their eyes they have closed; lest they should perceive with their eyes and hear with their ears . . ." (Isa. 6:9-10; cf. Acts 28:26-27). The sinner has eyes but does not see, ears and does not hear. Even more forcefully, Jesus tells those who "reject the light," "If you were blind, you would have no guilt; but now that you say, 'We see,' your guilt remains" (John 9:41).

A homely example may sharpen the point. My private project may be my success as a scholar. All my best energies are funneled into that goal from which I hope to gain life and worth. Like all such projects from which so much is sought, it has grown distended, more than a little idolatrous. Not only weekdays but also weekends, I labor over my books obsessively. Not even football can sway me from my books. But my five-year-old daughter calls me plaintively from the playroom, "Daddy, I'm lonesome. Come watch cartoons with me." In the most straightforward sense, my daughter has offered me the gift of otherness. It directly challenges my project. I must decide whether to maintain the project or let it go for the moment in order to accept the gift. In this case, I may decide to stick with my books, telling myself that I'll watch with her next Saturday. But if I choose to stick with my project *every time* my daughter calls, it is likely that eventually I will not hear her calling any more. I won't hear her because I have made my project so rigid that I am deaf to her call. And it is likely that I won't hear her because faced with multiple refusals, she has stopped calling. If I close myself to the other often enough, I can almost eliminate the other. But I am the one diminished.

In the same way, we as a society have our communal idolatry: We serve our comfort and prosperity. All our efforts go into maintaining our standard of living. But some citizens who share our space do not share our prosperity. By their very presence among us, they challenge our project and threaten our peace. They appear on street corners and in bus stations, in food lines and flophouses and halfway houses. They may even hold out their hands to us as we rush down the street. The dispossessed and disoriented among us offer otherness. They provide us the chance to grow into a larger view of the human condition than that shaped by sanity and safety, by comfort and pleasure. But if we refuse to see them, time after time, they will eventually disappear. They will disappear first because we will have grown blind to them. And they will literally disappear because our rigid project *will* eliminate them from society—by starvation, drugs, despair, and disease. Like idolatry, sin can be societal as well as individual.

Faith

Paul declares in Eph. 2:8, "you are saved by grace *through faith.* And this, not from yourselves but God's Gift; and not out of your efforts, lest anyone should boast" (author's translation). By faith Paul means the positive response of human freedom to the offer of God's grace. What was said above concerning sin should therefore apply also to faith. The word describes a dynamic process rather than a single act; a life-long pattern of response that finishes only with death.

If sin is to be defined in terms of closure and the refusal of God's gift, then faith is defined in terms of openness and the acceptance of that gift. Sin says no to otherness and its challenge to the constructed self; faith says yes to otherness and its call to grow into a project larger than that fashioned by fear and compulsion. Sin identifies reality with its own perception; even when offered another perspective, sin refuses to take this into account, choosing its old partial truth as the total truth. Faith allows the perception of the other to relativize its own perspective, just as it allows the project of another to relativize its own project.

Just as sin distorts the self and ultimately destroys it by isolation, so does faith save the self by enabling it to enter into a larger version of the truth, and by opening it to the true source of life and worth, the living God. So fundamental is this response to reality that we must discuss it at greater length.

5

The Life of Faith

*T*he central Christian symbol for the human response to God that is "righteous," that is, rightly aligned with the truth about God as creator and humans as creatures, is called faith. As with other concepts we have examined, it is better understood as a verb than as a noun, and as a process of responding to reality. The name first and most prominently used by Christians took this verbal form: they were *hoi pisteuontes*, "the faithers" (see, e.g., 1 Thess. 1:7; 2:13; Acts 2:44; 4:32). As a substantive, the term "faith" is used to describe the entire righteous human response to God's gift, in contrast to sin (see Rom. 14:23). It can therefore be used as shorthand to refer to the entire "Christian Thing" (e.g., Gal. 6:10).

Any symbol used so centrally and extensively accrues inevitable associations and nuances. It is helpful therefore to distinguish between the symbol's several aspects in order to discover the underlying unity that binds them together. I will first describe the multiple dimensions of the term faith. Then I will concentrate on the aspect of "faithing" as a verb which is the direct opposite of sin: faith as obedience. Finally, I will show how Jesus is both cause and exemplar of saving faith.

The Dimensions of Faith

The first dimension of faith is *belief*. Belief is the assent of the mind to certain convictions. When the creed states, "we believe in one

God," it contains an interpretation of reality as well as a personal commitment. The logical primacy of belief is stated by Heb. 11:6: "Without faith it is impossible to please him. For whoever would draw near to God must believe that he exists and that he rewards those who seek him." The content of this belief is spelled out earlier in Heb. 11:3, "By faith we understand that the world was created by the word of God, so that what is seen was made out of things which do not appear." This perception of reality is, we have seen, of fundamental importance. It makes the difference between perceiving the world as a closed system in which all creatures are in competition for limited resources, and perceiving it as open to a Giver of gifts from an endless font of life and power. Seen as open to a Creator, all creatures are regarded as equally gifted with being, equally known and loved by their Creator, whose resources can never be drained.

Belief should obviously translate itself into a consistent pattern of action, but it is possible to stop with the belief that there is a God and even to think that such an intellectual conclusion can save us. This faith without deeds is roundly condemned by the Letter of James: "You believe that God is one; you do well. Even the demons believe—and shudder . . . faith apart from deeds is useless" (James 2:19-20). The assent of the mind to abstract truths is an essential aspect of faith but it is not sufficient.

A second dimension of faith is *trust*. Considered as trust, faith shifts focus from the mind to the heart, from a set of concepts to a personal relationship. Thus, in secular Greek usage, I would entrust funds to the disposition of another because I trusted her. The word *pistis* (faith) would fit both action and attitude. With respect to God, then, faith means entrusting one's life to the disposition of the Creator. This is indeed a "leap" of faith, from an intellectual to an existential commitment. There is far greater risk involved in trusting God as a living power whose knowledge and love I now rely on, than in believing that there is a God.

Trust shows us the interpersonal nature of faith. I can believe a mathematical deduction, but I can properly and in the full sense trust only a person. By putting my trust in God's power and Word, I signal that I do not rely on my own. In the most vivid fashion, I acknowledge that I am contingent and dependent—I willingly lean on another for life. In the biblical story, trust is a critical element in Abraham's faith for which God declared him righteous. God promised Abraham a blessing, and Abraham "believed," that is, he trusted in and acted upon that promise (Gen. 15:5-6). My trust in God also implies, paradoxically, a certain trust in my self. If I can make this leap, I somehow trust my perception that there is something on the other side.

Another dimension of faith is *obedience*. In this dimension, my perception of God as Creator and my trust in God's power is translated into a pattern of life. So central is this dimension that Paul virtually equates the terms when he makes "the obedience of faith" thematic for his whole exposition in the Letter to the Romans (Rom. 1:5; 16:26). In the biblical tradition, faith as obedience means a deeply responsive hearing of God, a hearing that at some level says "yes" to God. Faith as obedience is demonstrated by Abraham's departure from his native land and possessions in response to God's call (Gen. 12:1-4), and above all by his willingness to sacrifice his only son Isaac in response to God's command (Gen. 22:19). This aspect of faith is in many ways the most central to a proper understanding of Christian maturity, and will need fuller development. For now, I simply note that faith as obedience is made exemplary for Christian existence not only by James (James 2:22-23) and the Letter to the Hebrews (Heb. 11:8-19), but also by Paul (Rom. 6:15-19). For Paul, the supreme exemplar of faith as obedience is not Abraham but Jesus (Rom. 5:12-21; Phil. 2:1-11).

A fourth dimension of faith is *hope*. This way of putting it may seem strange; we are accustomed to think of hope as a quality or disposition distinct from faith, as when Paul says, "There remain faith, hope, and love, but the greatest of these is love" (1 Cor. 13:13), or when he praises the Thessalonian Christians for their "work of faith and labor of love and steadfastness of hope" (1 Thess. 1:3). Yet, other texts make it clear that hope is a dimension of faith. Thus, the classic definition of faith in Heb. 11:1: "Faith is the assurance of things hoped for, the conviction of things not seen." So also Paul can refer to those who mourn their dead as acting "as those who have no hope," and go on to define the difference in terms of *faith*: "for since we believe that Jesus died and rose again, even so, through Jesus, God will bring with him those who have fallen asleep" (1 Thess. 4:13-14). Even more emphatically, in Paul's analysis of Abraham's faith, he says "in the presence of the God in whom he believed, who gives life to the dead and calls into existence the things that do not exist. In *hope he believed* against hope, that he should become the father of many nations, as he had been told" (Rom. 4:17-18).

It is difficult to define hope precisely. In effect, it is the attitude or disposition that enables us to move into the future. Functionally, hope is what gets us out of bed in the morning and enables us to get on with our day. It is the opposite of despair, which tells us to cut off the future by ending our life now. In the deepest sense, though, hope is less an expectation concerning the future (that such and such will happen) than a perception of the present which enables us to envisage and move into our future. Despair is the denial of faith for it looks only at our enslavement within our human projects, sees only that by ourselves, we are truly hopeless idolaters who turn every gift into a possession. Hope is a dimension of faith because it looks at the freedom that is constantly offered us by the God who graces us with the gift of otherness and provides us the chance to change.

A fifth dimension of faith is *fidelity*. The Greek word *pistos* ("faithful") signifies more than a believer. It means someone who is loyal. Fidelity means faithfulness in a relationship of belief, trust, hope, and obedience. Faith is not a single event, or a once-for-all decision. It is, rather, a response that is repeatedly renewed in each encounter with the Other in the world. Fidelity suggests the character-forming nature of the faith response, and the reason why the term "faith" can legitimately denote a virtue as well as a religious decision.

A proper grasp of this dimension of faith, however, involves understanding to what or to whom, as well as how one is faithful. It would be a mistake to think of fidelity as simple consistency, or sticking to one's own word. Indeed, loyalty to one's own past word or promise or record considered in itself may or may not be good. It can, in fact, represent a disastrous form of idolatry that can close us off to the recognition of the Other in our present circumstances.

Fidelity, therefore, is directed not to my self or my interpretation of the world, but to the Other whom I encounter through the multiple gifts of otherness in the world. And since these gifts are renewed at every moment of creation, my fidelity as well must have a *creative* component to it. I must respond to the world as it now presents itself to me, not as it formerly did, or as I thought it did. It was Paul's perception of his fellow Jews' failure to do this that motivated his criticism of them in Rom. 9:30—10:3. The problem is not that Jews did not have faith in God. Paul says clearly, "they have zeal for God but not according to recognition" (10:2). The problem arises only *with* the gift of the Messiah. Faced with this new revelation of God, they chose to be consistent with their own past (*and* their understanding of *God's* own past) rather than respond to this new dimension of righteousness displayed in a crucified Messiah. It is in that sense, not in the sense that Paul *or* his fellow Jews were hopeless legalists closed to God in every respect, that Paul states, "not recognizing the righteousness from God and seeking to stand on their own (understanding of) righteousness, they did not submit themselves to the righteousness of God" (Rom. 10:3). Fidelity is therefore flexible because it responds to the other *as* other through time.

A sixth dimension of faith in God is *perseverance*. This dimension is closely related to fidelity, but it points more directly to the inevitable note of suffering in faith, the fact that faith is not so much a *doing* as a letting be, and the truth that the process does not end until our death. This aspect of faith is particularly important precisely because the human spirit tends toward premature closure. We always want to end before the end. We want to have our lives as a product, a possession. We grow weary of having to respond to gift, we tire of always being in process. Faith as perseverance— or endurance—allows us, despite the fact that we close on every previous obedience as the last, to remain open again to the gift and call of God. This aspect of faith, that it *endures* to the end, is emphasized especially in Heb. 10:32-39 and James 5:7-11. James, in fact, declares, "Behold we call blessed those who endured" (5:11).

The seventh and final dimension of faith is *love*. As in the case of hope, and for similar reasons, calling love a dimension of faith may cause some surprise. I am not interested in flattening the richness of the Christian attitude called *agape* by reducing it to a subspecies of faith. Rather, I am concerned to show that we better understand *agape* when we see how it articulates faith. If *agape* means willing good for others not for our benefit but for theirs, we can see that it is faith which allows the other to be other, instead of an extension of our self-project. In *agape*, we simply reverse the direction of the pattern by which faith accepts the gift of being known and accepted by God, and offer the same gift to others. We seek their good not because we will thereby grow greater, but because, ultimately, God will be glorified.

To glorify God means recognizing God's implicit presence and power in the world, acknowledging God's claim on the world (see Rom. 1:21 and 4:20). When we allow other creatures to *be* other, we thereby implicitly recognize that they are God's creatures, not ours, that they are part of God's project, not ours, that they are obliged to God, not to us. We value them and seek their good not because they can do something for us or because they are particularly attractive, but because as God's creatures they indirectly reveal the Creator. When we therefore know them as other—that is, as they are and not as we would wish them to be—and when we love them as other—that is, as separate and worthwhile persons or beings whose existence and value does not derive from either us or themselves but the One who creates them at every moment—we implicitly both know and love God. Precisely this perception of the other is given uniquely by faith. Faith and love are aspects of the same overall response to reality by which we accept grace from God and by so doing become grace for others.

The Obedience of Faith

The dimension of faith most central to the biblical tradition is obedience. It is also the dimension which best fits my analysis of the human project of becoming a person. I ask the reader to recall how as humans engage the world, their encounter with God is always implicit and indirect. We do not encounter "the Other" as such, but only an implicit presence mediated by many separate others. If there is a "divine project" at work in the world (and it is faith's conviction that there is), we meet it not as something apart from the projects of other humans, but precisely through those projects. The free obedience of the human spirit to God, in short, is always and inevitably mediated through the response of the human spirit to the physical world and above all, other humans.

I have said that faith is a deeply responsive *hearing* of another by which a person overcomes the internal resistance of attachment to one's own project, and in some sense says yes to the project of another. Such faith requires three separate elements: a project of one's own to which there is a real commitment; the call of another which at once provides the gift of otherness but also threatens one's ongoing project; and, the relativization of one's project that occurs when the other is truly taken into account.

Even looked at in these simple terms, the difficulty of such obedience is obvious. To let go of my own project means to let go of my very self and self-perception, so every act of obedient faith is a passage from death to life. The larger life made possible by my yes to the other, furthermore, is not obvious, and requires both trust and hope. In passage, all that is apparent is the death. Such faith also inevitably involves *suffering* in its very structure; part of us dies, and dies painfully, when we stretch to a larger life, or make room within our hearts for a larger presence.

It is clear as well that there is no end to this response, for there is never (because of God's creation at every moment) any end to the others we must encounter. We are therefore caught in a constant tension. Our natural tendency (because of our need to center) is toward idolatry. Even when we allow our idolatrous project to be cracked open by allowing an Other in, we then want to close on *that* new project, that new definition of the self, and be done with it. But faith requires that we remain open to the next other that we meet. However many new openings we try to close—perhaps even manage to close—we will be challenged to open ourselves still again. We must live till death in an oscillation between idolatry and faith. Faith is never product, but always process. It is never achievement but always response to gift. It is never "our" project, but always the intrusion of the Other's project.

All of this would be bad enough, but still does not reveal the most profound difficulty in living out the obedience of faith, which is that we cannot ever be sure whether or how the "other" we encounter represents a call from the Other who is God. It would be silly to suggest that I must respond to every other with a yes to its project on its terms. Sometimes, indeed, my yes to the Other may require a no to this other whom I encounter here and now. Not everything that encounters me is good, or a call to growth. Some projects are evil, or erroneous, or only variations on my own idolatry.

My yes to the other must therefore be understood in terms of taking it into account, and allowing it to relativize my own project. My yes to the other must be, to state it as clearly as possible, not a yes to the other's own idolatrous project as it is expressed in desires and needs that are perhaps destructive of the other, but a yes to the other as God's precious creature. But what this means in terms of specific human decisions is not clear. Therefore *discernment* is an absolutely critical component in the obedience of faith. Discernment, however, is no more a product than is faith, but is equally a process of perception and interpretation, which must remain open to revision and can never assert ultimacy for itself. The true asceticism of the obedience of faith is the asceticism of *attentiveness*.

We come, then, to the genuinely risk-filled nature of obedient faith. We can never know in this life whether our decisions are the correct decisions. In hindsight, we can usually assess them fairly accurately. But hindsight is of notoriously little assistance when our decisions must be made here and now with the capacity to shape our future. In the decision itself we cannot know with certainty that our response is truly one of faith or of idolatry. The breathtaking freedom of the human spirit is vividly exposed by the obedience of faith. We walk on thin ice through our life. We are never able to guarantee the safety of our next step. Yet we are required to keep taking each step. We cannot at any point stop, for what may feel like solidity now beneath our feet is illusory, and cannot bear the weight we want to put on it.

A Process. There is also a profound comfort in this slippery passage. It is in this *process* itself that God finds our righteousness. It is "out of faith that the righteous person shall live" (Rom. 1:17). Doing God's will is not a matter of product but of process. God's will is not some sort of blueprint of right decisions sketched in a divine book, the doing of which or the failure to do which means reward or punishment. And even if there were such a blueprint, it is patently not available to any human scrutiny. Those who say otherwise are either lying or self-deluded. If we piled up all the prescriptions in Torah, all the commandments of Jesus, all the directions of Paul, all the letters of councils and popes, and all the codicils in canon law, they would cover only a small portion of the situations we face in our lives.

Doing God's will, therefore, is not a matter of doing one thing rather than another (although that is also involved in obvious ways) but rather is found in the *process* of deciding one way rather than another. It is possible for me to do "the right thing for the wrong reason," in which case I am manifestly not doing what God wills. It is also possible for me to do what appears at the moment to be against all precedent for God's will (such as worshiping a crucified Messiah) and be acting in faith that God deems righteous.

The understanding of faith as a process is found in Micah 6:6-8. The prophet responds to God's complaint that the people neglect him despite all that he had done for them. The prophet asks in his own voice, "With what shall I come before the Lord, and bow myself before God on high?" He wants to respond personally to the claim of God on all the people. The prophet then proposes several possible ways he could respond, according to how he understands God's desire. He offers first to make external sacrifices: he will donate year-old calves, thousands of rams, rivers of oil. These are the prophet's *possessions*, and his willingness to give them shows his readiness to acknowledge God as the giver of worth. Then, he proposes something far more drastic, the sacrifice of his firstborn for his transgression, "the fruit of my body for the sin of my soul." Here is another possession of the prophet, but one much more internal, a part of the prophet's own *life*.

But God refuses these products. What God wills is not a dramatic self-impoverishment much less a dramatic self-mutilation in single gesture, but a continuous human response to reality by which others can be enriched and made whole. God responds to the prophet, "He has showed you, O man, what is good; and what the Lord requires of you." It turns out that this requirement is not a thing, or a single gesture, but the whole process of living itself: "To do justice, and to love kindness, and to walk humbly with your God." These are verbs, not nouns, and they are all progressive. It is in faithing, the risk-filled adventure of human freedom, that God sees righteousness.

The Example of Abraham.   The structure of obedient faith can be traced above all in the biblical account of Abraham, whom Paul presents as the exemplar of righteousness, calling him "father of all faithers" (Rom. 4:11). Chapter 12 of Genesis begins abruptly: "The Lord said to Abram." The word of God encounters Abram suddenly and unexpectedly; it did not figure in his plans or project. We must supply out of the hints of Genesis 11 just how full Abram's previous life was. To respond to this naked call, he had to leave the land of his ancestors, his family, and his property; all the things that gave him, as to every human being, a sense of identity and security.

Above all, to answer this call he had to leave behind his ancestral gods, to obey a voice that offered him with no evidence or proof only a bare promise, "I will make you a great nation, and I will bless you." He was asked to become a wanderer in a hostile environment (just how hostile is shown in Genesis 14 and 19). Abraham did not give a speech or build an altar or organize or plan. In a response of stunning simplicity he obeyed: "Abram went as the Lord directed him." He left the life that was under his control, and committed himself in freedom. By going he stepped out of a world defined by himself into a wider world defined by the One who called him.

From this point on in the Genesis narrative the problem becomes: is the promise God made to Abraham going to be fulfilled, and if so, how? Abraham had taken the first step and done as the Lord commanded. But the fulfillment of the promise did not occur. Abram grew older and his wife Sarah remained barren. Abram could see no human hope for the promise to be kept. But he tried to do God's will by his own effort. He used the legal means allowed by ancient law to make Eliezer, the steward of his household, his legal heir (15:2-3). But then came a second and more mysterious visitation from God at the time of Abraham's uncertainty and desperation (15:1-5). Once more, the promise was not fulfilled, only renewed. And this time, *with all the human evidence to the contrary*, Abraham again believed. This faith in the face of counterevidence, this trust in God's power rather than his own, is what God counts as righteous in Abraham (15:6).

But precisely because the promise is made more clearly than ever, Abraham's problem becomes even greater. The narrator notes succinctly, "Abram's wife Sarah had borne him no children." Shouldn't he do something to help God's project along? Thinking once more that human resourcefulness can accomplish God's will, Abraham turns to his concubine Hagar and has a child by her (16:1-6). But in addition to creating a family crisis, Abraham has done nothing to advance the fulfillment of the promise. It must come by God's gift, not by human effort. Now, having reduced the human possibilities to nothing (adoption no good, concubinage no good, human parents impotent and barren), God reveals his own way of bringing about the promise: It is Sarah who is to have the son, after all (17:15-16).

God has led Abraham through all these plans, alternatives and frustrations to teach him that his faith must be in God, not in himself or in his project. And at last it looks as though there is to be a happy ending. Sarah will have the son of the promise. Abraham enjoys great intimacy with God: God visits his tents and shares Abraham's hospitality. Abraham speaks boldly with God face-to-face as mediator for the people of Sodom and Gomorrah. Truly, Abraham is the friend of God. Finally, the heir of the promise is born. "Abraham was a hundred years old when his son Isaac was born to him. And Sarah said, 'God has made laughter for me, everyone who hears will laugh over me.' And she said, 'Who would have said to Abraham that Sarah would suckle children? Yet I have borne him a son in his old age.' And the child grew, and was weaned,

and Abraham made a great feast on the day of the child's weaning"
(21:5-8). It appears at last as though all Abraham's problems are
over.

But what Abraham surely must have considered to be the end
and reward for his faith turns out to be only a plateau. God leads
him to a still more radical level of obedience. With great irony, the
narrator has the word come to Abraham in the same way as at his
original call: "Abraham." And steady Abraham answers, "I am here."
What the voice now demands, however, is so contrary to reason,
to moral sensibility, indeed, to *everything previous in his experience
of God*, that Abraham can only consider it absurd. Abraham is told
to sacrifice his son, Isaac.

This is no mere challenge to leave homeland, family, property,
and ancestral gods for the sake of something better that God will
give; this is the demand to kill the very gift that God has given! It
forces a "crisis of faith" in the truest sense. Abraham, after all, had
done what God demanded, guided only by the promise through
the ambiguities of his life. Now, with the cup of joy barely to his
lips, he is being asked to toss it away. Now there would be absolutely
no further possibility of having heirs. Had he imagined everything
that had gone before? Or worse, was God playing him for a fool?

The greatness of Abraham is shown in his silent obedience.
"Abraham rose early in the morning, saddled his ass, and took two
of his young men with him, and his son Isaac" (22:3). Abraham's
inner resistance to hearing and doing must have been enormous.
Here the pain of response, the suffering of saying yes, goes beyond
all reckoning. For three days they travel in silence. Abraham's interior
disposition is revealed only in the pathetic, ironic, dialogue between
the bewildered child and himself: "My father!" "Here am I, my son"
(answering this other as he does the Other). "Behold, the fire and
wood; but where is the lamb for a burnt offering?" "God will provide
himself the lamb for a burnt offering, 'my son.'" And at the critical
moment, God does provide, in a characteristically unexpected way.
Abraham has passed the test; he has followed the Word of God
into unspeakable darkness and despair, to the loss of everything he
held dear, only to receive it back again, as always received—not as
his possession, but as gift. This is the lesson.

It is customary—and an act of piety to Abraham—to end the
story at that point. But none of us can stop till death, and neither
could Abraham. He continued to negotiate for his possession of the

land (23:17-20) and for control of the blessing through the descendants of Isaac, arranging, arranging till the end: sending Isaac to marry a relative; giving all his possessions to Isaac but gifts to his other children through concubinage; sending these children "away from his son Isaac" so that the land would be his (25:1-6). Abraham, like us all, tried mightily to control the course of events. Neither could he maintain obedient faith as a "style of life." And all the hard lessons of whose land this was, and whose the power, and by what means the promise would be fulfilled had to be learned over again in the stories of Isaac and Jacob . . . and us. Only once do we find the pattern of faith enacted perfectly through life into death, and that is in the faith of Jesus, who, as Hebrews tells us, is not only the starter with respect to faith, but also the finisher (Heb. 12:3).

The Faith of Jesus

It is perfectly appropriate for Christians to speak of their "faith in Christ," as a way of specifying their particular response to God mediated by the crucified and raised Messiah Jesus. Such language is legitimated by the New Testament itself which speaks of "believing in Christ" (Gal. 2:16). But when such language is used exclusively it can obscure truths essential to the Christian experience.

It is somewhat misleading, for example, to say that one's faith is in Jesus, or that one relies on Jesus. The name Jesus, like the title Messiah, must be retained for the specific historical person. But the response of obedient faith has as its only appropriate object the One God. And if one means by faith in Christ simply a shorthand way of saying faith in God because, after all, "Christ is God," then one has confused important distinctions that Christian theologians of the first four centuries spent a great deal of effort to maintain. Worse, when the significance of Jesus' human response to God is slighted, then something of fundamental importance in the Christian understanding of *faith* has been lost.

For Paul, the Greek phrase *pistis Christou*, which most contemporary translations render as "faith in Christ," actually referred to the "faith of the Messiah," that is, the response to God in trust and obedience of the human person Jesus. This "faith of Jesus," furthermore, is understood by Paul to be precisely the means by which God's saving gift has been made available to other humans. Paul states this in compressed fashion in Gal. 2:16-21. He contrasts the quest for righteousness that stems from human effort (the project he calls "works of the law") with the gift of righteousness that comes from God "through the faith of Jesus Messiah" and "out of the faith of Messiah" (2:16). Spelling out the transforming gift from God, he says, "I live no longer myself but Christ lives in me. The life I lead in the flesh I live by the faith of the Son of God, who loved me and gave himself for me." For Paul, the obedience and love of Jesus *is* the gift of God's knowing and loving us.

Paul repeats this more elaborately in Romans. In Rom. 3:21-26, he describes the "gift of God" that reverses the systemic distortion of the world deriving from idolatry (1:18—3:20). God's gift to humans is the sacrificial death of his Son. But Paul interprets this sacrifice in terms of a free offering of the human Jesus, "through the faith of Jesus Christ," (3:22), "through faith" (3:25). And this gift not only shows that God is righteous but that he makes righteous those who "have the faith of Jesus" (3:26).

An Obedient Faith. The way Paul understands Jesus' human faith is precisely in terms of obedience. Having sketched the faith of Abraham as an example for Christians (Rom. 4:1-25), Paul elaborates the "gift of God" (5:15). He multiplies synonymous phrases to indicate that his subject is not the human response, but what *God* has done. He calls it the "grace of God and the free gift in the grace of that one man Jesus Messiah," which has now overflowed to many (5:15). The gift, Paul says, is found in the obedience shown toward God by this "one man" Jesus. It is his obedience that opens up the possibility of new life. In contrast to Adam's disobedience which began the reign of sin and death, Jesus' obedience establishes the possibility of "life eternal."

That Paul has in mind the human response of Jesus to God is made obvious by the passage in Phil. 2:1-11. Here, Paul explicitly presents the "mind of the Messiah" to his readers as an example. He explicates this messianic consciousness in terms of Jesus' radical obedience to God. He did not count equality with God something to be seized; he took the form of a servant; as a servant, he was obedient, even to death; this is the reason God exalted him and gave him an identity as Lord that is above all others. I will return at the end of this chapter to the way Paul applies this messianic pattern as a model for his readers' own faith.

The Letter to the Hebrews places an equally great emphasis on the obedient faith of Jesus. Hebrews understands Jesus as open to doing God's will from the moment of his human birth: "When Christ came into the world he said . . . I have come to do thy will, O God, as it is written of me in the roll of the book" (Heb. 10:5-7). At the same time, Hebrews stresses the intense involvement of the Messiah in the human condition: "Since, therefore, the children share in flesh and blood, he himself likewise partook of the same nature . . . he had to be made like his brethren in every respect. . . . Because he himself has suffered and been tempted, he is able to help those who are tempted" (2:14-18). Also, "We have not a high priest who is unable to sympathize with our weaknesses, but one who in every respect has been tempted as we are, yet without sin" (4:15).

The obedience of Jesus, in other words, was neither automatic or easy; he was tested as we are. Hebrews, in fact, offers us a powerful image of how painful this response was for the human person Jesus: "In the days of his flesh, Jesus offered up prayers and supplications, with loud cries and tears, to him who was able to save him from death, and he was heard for his godly fear. Although he was a Son, he learned obedience through what he suffered; and being made perfect, he became the source of eternal salvation of all who obey him" (5:7-9).

The statements of Hebrews are of extraordinary importance because they show us that the faith of Jesus was a process that continued through his life; a process that involved being tested or tempted by projects other than the one willed by God, that involved relativizing his own desire to live, that meant tears and agony. And Hebrews tells us that it was precisely in this process that he became "perfected," that is, mature. Hebrews says, "It was fitting that he, for whom and by whom all things exist, in bringing many sons to glory, should make the pioneer of their salvation perfect (mature) through suffering" (Heb. 2:10). The key here is the conviction that obedient faith is itself a form of suffering. Hebrews is familiar with the Greek proverb, *mathein pathein*, "to learn it is necessary to suffer." It applies this to Jesus: by his obedience, he learned to be son, and it hurt. Hebrews applies the same lesson to Christians: "You endure for the sake of an education" (12:7).

From Hebrews we learn that Jesus' human spirit progressively opened itself to the presence and power of God by the painful response of obedient faith. He progressively *became* obedient Son in the course of his life, so that his death, which appeared as a final closure, actually became an opening of his spirit to the Spirit of God; and more, an opening for all other humans to follow, "the new and living way which he opened for us through the curtain, that is, through his flesh" (10:19). By his death and resurrection, he was "finished" in this process, and not before: "being made perfect he became the source of eternal salvation to all who obey him" (5:9). And as cause he is also example so that Christians who are called to faith and obedience and in that response inevitably experience pain and suffering can "look to Jesus, the pioneer and perfecter of faith" (12:3).

Paul and the author of Hebrews make explicit by way of proposition what is implicit in the story of Jesus. They wrote—almost certainly—before the Gospels were composed, but they articulated for their readers the meaning of the story that was already shared in the churches. The convictions of faith in turn shaped the image of Jesus we now find in the Gospels. This makes them all the more valuable to us as we look to Jesus to discover what the obedience of faith might mean, and read the Gospels to discover the messianic mind that Paul says should be ours.

The Faith of Jesus.   The story of Jesus' testing in the wilderness shows us something of the pattern of his faith. Mark summarizes the fact in two verses (Mark 1:12-13); Matthew and Luke elaborate it into a disputation between Jesus and Satan involving the interpretation of Torah (Matt. 4:1-11; Luke 4:1-13) . Although the scene is highly stylized in the Synoptic Gospels, and is presented immediately after Jesus' baptism as a sort of paradigmatic event, the fourth Gospel provides intimations of the same sort of testings throughout Jesus' ministry, suggesting perhaps that Jesus' struggle to respond to God's project was not a quick or easy one (see John 6:14-15; 7:3-4; 11:27-28).

At issue is the sort of Messiah Jesus was to be. As a native of Galilee in the revolutionary turmoil of first century Palestine, Jesus could not but have been sympathetic to his fellow Jews' longing for a liberator. To be a military messiah, a zealot leader, to exercise visible and dramatic power, to control events—this was a real possibility for a personality as charismatic as Jesus.

The temptation account makes clear, however, that in his days of prayer, reflecting over his own experience and desires in the light of Torah, Jesus discovered the path he must follow; not the obvious way of human greatness and power, but the way of the suffering servant. He would not organize a militia or establish an alternative kingdom. He was to live "by every word that proceeds from the mouth of God," to "not tempt the Lord," and to "worship the Lord (his) God, him only (to) serve" (Matt. 4:4, 7, 10).

The temptation accounts show that Jesus' mission as Messiah was not to be one of willful activity, but one of responding to the moment's needs, of remaining open to the call of God as it came to him in the needs of the others he encountered every day. The faith of Jesus meant to say "Yes" to the Father in the concrete circumstances of his life, thus fashioning in his flesh a path that every person could follow.

The stereotypical nature of the temptation accounts are revealed when we read between the lines of Mark's narrative. Surely not a biography but a witness and interpretation of Jesus' identity, the narrative reveals—perhaps unwittingly, perhaps by literary or divine inspiration—the structure of human faith in the way it tells Jesus' story. Read this way, it becomes clear that the issue of what Jesus was to do was not answered once for all, and remained a struggle. Each time he formed a project, it was challenged by the Other.

We are given one striking example in the sequence of Mark 1:29-45. The response to Jesus' initial preaching and exorcism is a constant press of people seeking healing (1:29-32). The next morning, Jesus rises early to pray; he wants to be alone. His disciples follow him and tell him everyone seeks him (for healing). Jesus rejects that challenge in light of his understanding of God's mission: "Let us go on to the next town, that I might preach there also, for that is why I came." Jesus' project (which is his understanding of God's will) is to preach, not heal, so he follows that project, "preaching . . . and casting out demons" (1:39). *The very next story* in Mark shows the intrusion of an other; a leper asks to be made clean. In order to respond to this gift/challenge from the other, Jesus must relativize his own project. He does so, and cleanses the leper.

But see the result! The man who was formerly ostracized from society ends up "talking freely about it." And Jesus? He could no longer openly enter a town but was out in the country. The result of his response of faith was unexpected, and led to a far more drastic change of his life than he could have anticipated. The unexpected reversal went even further: "People came to him from every quarter" (1:45). What Jesus wanted was to preach or to pray alone. What he got was removal from preaching and a crowd seeking healing.

This sequence shows us the forming of a human project by Jesus, his attempt to follow it, his openness to the other's needs and willingness to let go of his project, and the change in his life as a consequence.

A similar narrative sequence is found in Mark 6:30-56; by reading it we come to understand more fully what it means to be open to the call of God in the needs of others. Jesus had sent the Twelve on mission (6:7-29). When they returned, he told them, "Come away by yourselves to a lonely place, and rest a while." The evangelist notes, "For many were coming and going, and they had no leisure even to eat" (6:30-31). The situation is almost identical to the earlier one: Jesus and his followers are harassed by those who are needy, and cannot tend to their own basic needs. Jesus therefore shapes a reasonable project of self-protection; he and his friends will withdraw and rest. They not only formed a desire, they put it in action: "And they went away in the boat to a lonely place by themselves" (6:32).

It was not to be. The people followed them, even arriving at the "lonely spot" before Jesus and the Twelve. "As he went ashore he saw a great throng." Here, we need to imagine the emotional response caused by such a disappointment, and the implicit demand placed on a weary man (we should say, perhaps, a burnt-out man) by this never-ending needy mob. But Jesus is "moved with compassion" and responds to their need. He teaches them the whole day. Then, another crisis: the crowd needs feeding. The one who wanted to retire with friends for a picnic lunch finds himself the host for five thousand—with no mention of him eating, at all (6:24-44).

The "Yes" of Jesus to the Father was not always filled with pain. There is the moment of ecstasy recorded by Matthew and Luke, when Jesus, seeing the response of the crowds to his proclamation, "rejoiced in the Holy Spirit and said, 'I thank thee, Father, Lord of heaven and earth, that thou hast hidden these things from the wise and understanding and revealed them to babes'; yea, Father, for such was thy gracious will" (Luke 10:21; Matt. 11:25-27). The gift of otherness was sometimes unexpected joy.

The faith of Jesus, however, could not rest with any response. Jesus could not make final and ultimate any Yes until the last one. In the portrayal of Jesus in the garden before his arrest, trial, and death, Mark shows us the entire structure of obedient faith. We hear first, "Abba, Father, all things are possible to thee." Here is faith as belief and as trust. Jesus recognizes his creaturely dependence, and the power of God. But his commitment is personal. God is Father, indeed, "poppa." Jesus turns to God in his deepest emotional distress for relief. Second, we hear Jesus' own project clearly stated: "Remove this cup from me." Jesus does not want to die. His project is to live. He asks God to enable his project to succeed. But then, we hear the essential note of obedience, "yet not what I will but what you will" (Mark 14:36). Jesus allows his own project to be relativized by the project of God, which will emerge in the terrible sequence of his own abandonment and death. Precisely at this moment do we understand the significance of Paul's statement concerning Jesus, "For the Son of God, Jesus Christ . . . was not Yes and No; but in him it is always Yes. For all the promises of God find their yes in him. That is why we utter the Amen through him, to the glory of God" (2 Cor. 1:19-20).

Jesus' Faith and Ours

It is important to note that we have discerned not simply isolated incidents in the life of Jesus, but the fundamental messianic pattern: Jesus' obedient faith in God, mediated by the needs of others. This is the pattern that the Spirit of Jesus is to enact in our lives, in the entirely different circumstances within which each of us exists. "Because you are sons, God has sent the Spirit of his Son into our hearts, crying, 'Abba! Father!' " (Gal. 4:6). Paul provides the behavioral corollary to this gift: "If we live by the Spirit, let us also walk by the Spirit" (5:25). And what does this mean, specifically? "Bear one another's burdens, and thus fulfill the Messianic Norm [*nomos Christou*, Law of Christ]" (Gal. 6:2).

We can now return to Paul's plain exposition of this in Philippians. We have seen how he quotes the hymn of the obedient Messiah to his readers, urging them to have this mind of Christ among them. To understand how the pattern of Jesus is to function in the community, we must begin our reading with the verses that immediately precede the hymn. Paul translates the vertical response of Jesus to the Father into a behavioral norm for the horizontal responses of community members toward each other. This is how they have "participation in the Spirit" (Phil. 2:1). He tells them that they are to be "in full accord and of one mind." But we would misread this if we understood it to mean that they had all to agree on everything beforehand, or all share exactly the same perspective on every issue. Not only is that patently impossible for any community, it would also negate the very interaction Paul encourages.

Rather, Paul calls for a certain attitude, what he calls "the mind which you have in Christ Jesus," and which he calls elsewhere simply, "the mind of Christ" (1 Cor. 2:16). What does he mean by this messianic perception? First, they are not to have selfishness or conceit. These are the attitudes associated with idolatry, which make each person's individual project absolute, and by which I can assert my own will at the expense of others. Rather, they are to have "lowliness of spirit." What does this mean? He explains at once, but the Greek phrase is so difficult to translate almost any rendering is a distortion: he says, "count others better than yourselves." This certainly does not mean "think of yourself as of less worth than others." It means instead, "in action, defer to others as having a better claim." And what this means Paul makes perfectly clear in the next line: "Let each of you look not only to his own interests, but also to the interests of others" (Phil. 2:4). Paul does not call for a will-less submersion in the projects of others. Instead, he requires that each person *have* an interest, or what I have termed a project. But neither can each person assert that project willfully over others, and dominate them. The messianic attitude is found rather in the willingness to relativize one's own project in light of that of others. A healthy community of faith, in turn, is one that enables this to happen.

Part Two

Connecting

6

The Prayer of Faith

I will now develop some of the practical implications of my understanding of Christian maturity. As we move from theory to
practice, it is appropriate to situate the life of the Spirit more directly
between the compelling alternative visions of Christian maturity—
which I have called respectively the gnostic and liberation models.

The first articulation of faith is prayer. Prayer is not simply one
expression of faith among others. In a very real sense, it is part of
the essential structure of faith. Prayer is, consequently, as multiform
and flexible as faith itself. Its practice is not dictated by theory but
by the movement of the Holy Spirit, "who apportions to each one
individually as he wills" (1 Cor. 12:11). My purpose here, therefore,
is not to distinguish between proper and improper forms of prayer,
or to give directions how to pray.

My purpose is rather to reflect on the *function* of prayer in the
life of faith. Prayer, like play, is something that we do for its own
sake, not because we hope to achieve something; it is purposeless
but meaningful activity. We do not pray with pragmatic results in
mind. But the very act of prayer serves a function within the life
of faith. This function derives not from the intentions of the one
who prays, but from the nature of prayer. I will discuss in turn
public worship and private contemplative prayer. Each is an indis-
pensable articulation of faith.

The gnostic model of spirituality finds private prayer its most
perfect expression, for this spirituality is all about the cultivation of

the inner self, the withdrawal from the world and physical reality. Spirituality is the leap of the soul to God's spirit in ecstasy. Contemplation is the heart of the gnostic model.

That model can, however, find but little place for public worship. Mystics have always had trouble with public structures and ritual. Worship involves bodies, first of all, and many of them. It involves formal structure and often a distribution of roles. Mystics worry about the formalism of liturgy and its resistance to interiority. They think that when Jesus declared a worship "in spirit and truth" (John 4:23), he meant it should take place in the recesses of the individual's soul. Public worship swallows up the individual in the group. It is at best a distraction, at worst an offense.

The liberation model, in contrast, finds no use for contemplation. Private prayer is useless (God is in fact found in social engagement) and even dangerous, since spirit-cultivation can lead to an alienation from the *praxis* of the movement. Contemplation is bad precisely because it is a withdrawal from action, and done in private.

The liberation model can make room for public worship, but only in a limited way. If worship is understood as a kind of group consciousness-raising and mobilizing of energy for action, then it has value. But this value depends on the degree to which it reinforces the ideology of the group. If worship is directed to an "Other" rather than to our own collective project, then it has the same problem as private prayer; it is a form of alienation. This is why the liberation model must be so preoccupied by the ideological consistency of public prayers, and the ideological purity of the Scripture texts read in the assembly. Texts that offend a community's religious, social, moral, or political proclivities must be censored. We cannot have anything read to us that conflicts with our own presuppositions, for the whole purpose of liturgy is to reinforce our commitment to that ideology.

But the life of faith that responds to the One God in the circumstances of worldly existence needs both public worship and contemplative prayer. Each serves a distinct and irreducible role.

Public Worship

The liberation model is certainly correct in thinking that one of the main functions of public worship is to reinforce a people's identity. When Christians come together in assembly, we articulate in a way not otherwise available that we *are* a people, a social entity. We state by the words we read, the things we say, and the gestures we make, that we are a people defined in terms of these symbols and rituals. But when we come together as a people, we also place ourselves in a position to be addressed by an Other, to be gifted by the call of God. The liturgy is quite literally the people's sacrament of encounter with God. Thus, each aspect of the liturgy gifts us with otherness, offers us as a people an identity that none of us individually can comprehend in thought or action. In the texts of Scripture that we hear read aloud to us, we are offered—however fragmentarily—a Word that escapes our manipulation. Here we are, locked in a pew; we cannot move; we must listen to words that are not our own. The closed circuit of my fantasy life, the compulsive round of my idolatrous project are interrupted by the voice of the prophet, the challenge of the gospel. We have Scripture read to us not only to have our self-image reinforced, but even more to have it challenged.

The Word in all its forms tells us the truth about our condition: that we are not self-sufficient, that we are creatures responsible for our lives to the One who creates us and knows us as we are. By so telling us this truth, the Word gifts us with the possibility of saying "yes"—if only momentarily—to a larger truth than the one we ordinarily tell ourselves, and so offers us a tiny opening to freedom within which God's Spirit can work.

But only if the texts are read to us in their integrity can they perform this function. If we rig the game, then they cannot speak to us as other. If we organize the texts and music only to create a certain emotional response or practical action, then we have engaged in a higher form of advertising or a less honest form of propagandizing. If we censor texts or alter them, so that they uniformly say what we want them to say, then we have merely made the texts speak with our own voice. We have again closed the circuit. There is no possibility for the Other to reach us in the texts and challenge us to growth and change, because the texts themselves are in no fashion other—they are simply our own voice in a different medium. The ideal, therefore, is to use a lectionary. Its construction also reflects a certain element of manipulation, it is true. But at least it comes to *us* as other, and not as a direct expression of our own ideology.

Of course some texts are hard for us to hear. Of course some texts seem to us scandalous. Of course we may need at some point to say no to what we understand as the import of some texts of Scripture. The same thing applies here as to the response of faith in our lives: not every other project demands a yes. But if we are to respond in faith, the other project must be heard, must be taken into account. Just as in our lives it is the task of discernment to weigh the options presented us by the other, so in the liturgy it is the task of preaching to *discern* the commanding Word of God in the disparate human words of the Bible. In the life of faith, however, this is one certainty: we cannot systematically close off the chance even to hear the other's project. So also in worship: we sin when by altering or manipulating the texts we deliberately close off the possibility of Scripture addressing us in the assembly. This is a deliberate deafness.

The recitation of the creed serves a similar faith-identity function. When we recite aloud together as a people the Rule of Faith, several important things happen simultaneously. We take to ourselves words that do not originate from ourselves; the creed was fashioned in the early history of our community and has come down to us by tradition, handed on by communities before ours who were shaped by it into their identity as God's people. Even as we speak, therefore, we are in this case hearing others. But because we also speak, we make those words our own; our voices give physical existence to our convictions; we assert before all the others with us and to ourselves that we choose to enunciate these symbols as the symbols by which we live.

Yet, these words are "other" to us in still another sense. Even as we say, "we believe," each of us knows the ways in which "*I* do *not* believe" that God is my Creator, perhaps, or that Jesus will come again. The words we speak as church stand over against each of us as challenge far more than as accomplishment. Finally, however, there is another sense in which we as a community *do* believe what each one of us as an individual cannot. Therefore we speak the creed together as a communal witness; each of us falls short of realizing faith in our lives; each of us oscillates constantly between idolatry and faith. But as a people we allow these words to express our shared conviction and the pattern by which we choose to live our lives. The church believes more and better than I do.

Public worship not only reflects our identity; it shapes our identity. Our worship not only gives us a model *of* our lives, it sketches a model *for* our lives. Nowhere is this more evident than in the Lord's Supper. In the ritual of bread and wine, we remember the words of Jesus before his death, the words by which he interpreted his own existence in terms of radical obedience to God and self-donating love for us. By eating the blessed bread and drinking the consecrated wine, we as a people literally take into ourselves the symbol by which we live. We take to ourselves the mystery of the Lord's death and resurrection as the normative meaning of our own passage through death to new life. This is indeed worship in spirit and in truth because the work of the Spirit is precisely to replicate in humans the pattern of Jesus the Messiah, the truth of humanity before God.

In an even more dramatic way, public worship is an occasion of grace for the very reasons it is a scandal to gnostic spirituality. In the liturgy we function as bodies and not simply as spirits: we stand and sit, kneel and march, shout and sing, sweat and snore. And we do this among other bodies, different from and perhaps even distasteful to us. Not everyone is beautiful or intelligent or quiet. Not everyone sings on key or in time. Babies cry, wheelchairs block the aisles, my pew companion has sweaty hands and halitosis.

And we, all together as bodies, confront the vagaries of official worship; aesthetically distressing garments; trite hymns; embarrassing readings; inept musicians and choirs; mumbling readers; poorly prepared preachers. Everything about this challenges our sense of propriety: the assembly is distressingly democratic and the worship alarmingly hieratic. We are assaulted by otherness. Our sense of privacy and interiority is threatened. We are constantly distracted from our private project of loving God in our hearts by the demands of this mob with its formal, messy, external show. Yes, exactly, and that is the point, that is the grace.

In liturgy, the Word of God does not only come to us in the otherness of text and creed and ritual. It confronts us literally and directly as it does every day of our lives—but now inescapably— in the intrusive presence of other persons. The liturgy is an articulation of faith because in it we are called out of our private project of idolatrous worship (God and me) to the larger project of a people shaped by God's Word. We are graced dramatically by the otherness of people, and thereby with the Otherness of God's Spirit. We are challenged to the task that Paul calls "discerning the body" (1 Cor. 11:29), by which he means more than recognizing the presence of the Lord in the sacrament of the bread and wine; he means recognizing the Lord in the sacrament that is this assembly of worshipers, the body of the Messiah.

Our capacity to say "yes, amen" to this offer of grace, as a people and as individuals within this people, gives us our identity as a community of faith and imprints each of us leaving this assembly with the messianic pattern by which we can discern the word in our individual daily lives. The liturgy is sacrament in the strict sense because it is the symbol and the reality of grace. No wonder it is the most precious articulation of faith for the people as a whole, in whatever season both a celebration of its identity and a glorification of God. How expressive of the right human posture before God is the dialogue between presider and people before the eucharistic prayer: "Lift up your hearts to the Lord." "We have lifted them up." "Let us give thanks to the Lord our God." "It is right to give him thanks and praise!"

Christians find an example for this articulation of faith both in Jesus and in the first believers. The Gospels show us Jesus frequenting the synagogues of Galilee (see Mark 1:39; 3:1; 6:2) and teaching in the precincts of the Temple in Jerusalem (see Luke 19:47; 20:1; 22:53). In Luke's powerful rendition of Jesus' rejection at Nazareth, we see how the reading of the Prophet Isaiah was taken by Jesus as defining his own messianic identity and mission (Luke 4:16-21). The very first converts in Jerusalem give themselves to "the breaking of bread and the prayers" (Acts 2:42). Furthermore, "attending the temple together and breaking bread in their homes, they partook of food with glad and generous hearts, praising God" (2:46-47). Such meetings "to break bread" continued in the church (Acts 20:7), and were recognized as essential for the realization of the church as a community of faith (see 1 Cor. 11:17-33). So we read the exhortation of Hebrews for those who "look to Jesus": "Let us consider how to stir up one another to love and good works, not neglecting to meet together, as is the habit of some, but encouraging one another, and all the more as you see the Day drawing near" (Heb. 10:24-25).

The Prayer of Individuals

The public worship of the community is extended by the verbal prayers of Christians in the multiple contexts of their lives. The Spirit leads each believer into modes of prayer appropriate to the temperament and situation of each, so that no experience of life need be excluded from prayer. At times, it is the prayer of blessing that seems most fitting, as we recognize the work of God in the world. This sort of prayer is deeply embedded in the biblical tradition and in the piety of Judaism. It is found in the mouth of Jesus, "I thank thee Father, Lord of heaven and earth" (Matt. 11:25), and in the letters of Paul, "God who is over all be blessed forever. Amen" (Rom. 9:5).

At other times, the prayer of petition is most apt, as we place before our Creator with open vulnerability our desire and need, asking that what we want be also what God wants, but always, that what God wants be done. Petitionary prayer is commanded by Jesus: "Ask, it will be given you; seek, and you will find; knock, and it will be opened to you" (Matt. 7:7). The prayer taught us by Jesus himself clearly contains the element of petition: "Give us this day our daily bread, . . . deliver us from evil (Matt. 6:11, 13). But the Lord's Prayer also contains, in a position of greater importance, the essential qualifier to all prayer of petition, "Thy kingdom come," which is understood to mean, "Thy will be done, on earth as it is in heaven" (Matt. 6:10). This is the structure also of Jesus' prayer in the garden, which perfectly expresses the nature of obedient faith: God's power is recognized ("All things are possible to Thee"); his own project is clearly stated ("remove this cup from me"); he allows God's project to relativize his own ("yet not what I will but what thou wilt" [Mark 14:36]).

Without this openness to God's project, petitionary prayer can creep dangerously close to magical manipulation. The words of Jesus, "It will be given" are sometimes interpreted to mean that if we ask long enough or hard enough, *what we want* will happen, as though faith were a matter of technique or sheer stubbornness. I suggest that if we take the words of Jesus more seriously, we find that they do *not* tell us that we will get what we ask for, but rather, "the good things" that God intends for his creatures (Matt. 6:11). And these good things may not in fact fit our own project.

The risk in petitionary prayer is that when we really "ask" God, we open ourselves to surprising and often paradoxical answers. The Letter of James castigates what he terms a "wicked" sort of prayer: "You ask and you do not receive because you ask wickedly, to spend on your own desires" (James 4:3). Prayer that is simply another effort to establish our own project in the world is idolatrous. James calls such a person "double-minded," because he or she seeks to live by two measures at once, with a heart divided: God's help is sought, but only on our terms. This is not an appropriate attitude with which to approach the Ruler of the universe, "from whom every good and perfect gift comes," and who, James reminds us, "gives to all people generously and without reproach" (James 1:5). The prayer of petition therefore must be "in faith" (James 1:6), which means that even as we offer our need and desire, we open ourselves to the better discernment of the One who sees the mind and the hearts of all, and therefore knows better than we do the good things we need.

In prayers of blessing and petition, the ordered verbal nature of prayer is obvious. It is clear that we not only lift up the heart but also lift up the mind to God. But humans are not always capable of speaking clearly who they are, what they feel or want; and at times it is necessary simply to make noises before the Lord. Sometimes these are joyful noises; as James says, "is any cheerful? Let him sing praise" (James 5:13). Sometimes they are rapturous noises, as in the Spirit-gifted, structured babble that is glossolalia (1 Cor. 12:10). Sometimes they are the inarticulate groans of suffering: "the cries of the harvesters have reached the ears of the Lord of hosts" (James 5:4), and "Jesus, Son of David, have mercy on me" (Mark 10:47).

All of these noises are authentic prayer; indeed, perhaps purer prayer for not being controlled by our rational, verbal projects, and for corresponding to our true condition before God. This assurance from Paul, therefore, is deeply comforting: "Likewise the Spirit helps us in our weakness; for we do not know how to pray as we ought, but the Spirit himself intercedes for us with sighs too deep for words. And he who searches the hearts of men knows what is the mind of the Spirit, because the Spirit intercedes for the saints according to the will of God" (Rom. 8:26-27).

The Prayer of Silence

Up to this point, I have considered the forms of prayer shared by all Christians. Each is an articulation of faith, each an expression of the life of the spirit, and therefore part of the spiritual life. Now it is time to consider the form of prayer which is sometimes regarded as virtually identical to the spiritual life, namely silent or contemplative prayer.

From early in the Christian tradition, some believers sought in the command of the Apostle, "Pray without ceasing" (1 Thess. 5:14), the essential mark of perfection. How could the life of faith be given fuller expression, they reasoned, than in a life totally committed to an explicit relationship with the object of faith, with God? And where could this relationship be better nurtured than in solitude and silence? There God could be met directly, rather than through the messy mediation of others. Much of the impulse behind the monastic "flight from the world" (*fuga mundi*) was this "desire for the face of God." The hermit could concentrate utterly on the "one thing . . . needful" (Luke 10:42). And if not many could bear quite that fevered a focus, then a monastic community could structure a way of life in which contemplation not only played an important role but was in many ways the community's reason for existing.

The more dramatically one committed oneself to contemplation, it was thought, the more seriously one took the spiritual life. Indeed, theologians were willing to rank life-styles on just such a basis, so that the contemplative life was superior to the active life because it had God as its explicit focus. Why was contemplation so highly regarded? Partly because of what is thought to happen in this form of prayer. Mysticism offers an unmediated religious experience. The mystic seeks unity with the divine, and the struggle to reach that state of unity involves all of the agony and doubt suggested by the "dark night of the soul." The mystic also seeks unification of the self. These two kinds of unity can obviously be related. Sometimes the true self is imagined as participating in the divine, so that reaching one means attaining the other as well. Sometimes, the quest for the face of God is thought to reveal a sense of the self that is more solidly grounded than the epiphenomenal ego defined by ordinary profane life.

Within this framework, Christianity through the centuries generated countless mystics who, in many different styles and points of emphasis, provided guidance to others through the classic stages of contemplative prayer: the purgative way, the illuminative way, and the unitive way. No period of Christianity was more prolific in this development than the centuries immediately before and after the Reformation, when the formalism of the liturgy and the hierarchy drove the creative spirit to an extravagant mystical expression in the lives of many: in England, the author of the *Cloud of Unknowing*, and Richard Rolle, Margery Kempe, and Julian of Norwich; in Spain, Theresa of Avila and John of the Cross and Ignatius of Loyola; in Germany, Jacob Boehme.

Even today, the popular understanding of spirituality is that it concerns the cultivation of the contemplative life. The notion persists that the best spirituality is available to those who can structure their existence around silence and solitude rather than to those who must labor amid the complexities of worldly existence. *Lay* spirituality often appears as the attempt to inject some element of this higher way of life into a profane existence, which means, in effect, imitating (always at some distance) the methods of the monks.

Since I lived the monastic life for many years and am still nostalgic for many of its attractions, I have no interest in denying the power or the beauty of the contemplative way as such. The reclusive and the monastic life are not only legitimate expressions of Christian identity, it can be argued that they are essential members in a healthily functioning body of Christ. But I am concerned with the lingering perception that hermits and monks are better Christians, or that the life of the Spirit demands imitating them. I am even more concerned with the emphasis in lay spirituality on silence and contemplation that bypasses its connection to the overall life of faith, either by the implicit suggestion that it is easy to experience God in prayer (despite the unanimous testimony of the great mystics directly to the contrary), or that the point of prayer is the establishment of a better rhythm to our lives (so that contemplation or meditation becomes a cheap form of psychotherapy).

I think it important to make and then develop three basic points about the prayer of silence. First, it is not a specialized activity for people of a certain temperament or even a particular spiritual charism; rather, the prayer of silence is an essential aspect of faith for all Christians. Second, it is not a complicated activity involving elaborate methods or techniques; rather, it is as simple as stopping, sitting, and shutting up. Third, it is not something that is done for its immediate payoff (because it is a neat experience) or for the sake of our psychic well-being (because it relieves our stress); rather it is a necessary precondition to our obedience of faith in the world.

Essential for All.   First, the prayer of silence is not an optional piece of piety for those who are dreamy or introverted, but an essential aspect of faith for all God's people. It does not require living in a structure organized to facilitate it. We do not flee the world in order to practice prayer; rather we pray in order to engage the world. We do not pray in an attempt to touch reality apart from others; rather we pray so that we are able to perceive reality truly in our encounter with others.

When we look to Jesus in the Gospel of Luke, which of all the Gospels pays greatest attention to prayer as a movement of the Spirit, we see that apart from his extended sojourn in the desert (4:1-13), Jesus' prayer is mentioned as an element throughout his ministry at every critical juncture. At his baptism he was praying (3:21); before he chose the Twelve, "he went out to the mountain to pray; and all night he continued in prayer to God" (6:12). Before Peter's confession of him as Messiah, Jesus was praying (9:18), and in the transfiguration he was praying (9:28-29). He prayed when he sent his missionaries out (10:21) and before teaching his disciples to pray (11:1). He prayed that Simon not fail (22:32) and that he himself might not die (22:41-42); and he ended his life in prayer: "Father, into your hands I commend my spirit" (23:46). When Paul tells us to "pray constantly" (1 Thess. 5:16) he does not mean to engage in it constantly as an activity to the neglect of living, but rather that prayer should be part of the process of our life of faith continuing until death. As it was for Jesus, so for those in whom the Spirit replicates the pattern of the Messiah.

How to Pray.   The prayer of silence, second, is not so complicated that it is unavailable to ordinary people. It is, as I have said, as simple as stopping, sitting down, and shutting up. By using these three terms, I am not prescribing a "method" of prayer. I am simply trying to show how simple is its essential structure; simple, of course, does not imply easy. By *stopping*, I mean that we deliberately cease our daily round of activity for a period of time. What is critical here is not the length of time but the reality of the stopping. We cannot pray and figure our taxes simultaneously, or talk on the phone. Stopping to pray does not mean taking out a few minutes to plan the rest of our schedule. Rather, it is stopping. For a moment, we exchange activity for being. We need to stop, because our *bodies* need to be involved. We allow our bodies to stand in witness to the world (if anyone is interested) but more importantly to ourselves, that we do not identify our being with our having, doing, and making; that we are not simply the same as our (inevitably idolatrous) project of the moment; that somewhere inside of us we know that our life is a gift and not a production. Stopping is the first and greatest risk of prayer, for it is an act of trust: we will not cease existing if we cease running, we will not become worthless if we cease from making things.

Then, we sit down. It does not matter, of course, whether we literally *sit*, but that is the body language most consonant with stopping. If we walk, we might start calculating how far we have walked and how many calories we have burned; if we walk, we might start jogging, saying to hell with it, I don't have time for both prayer and exercise today, so I'll combine them. If we kneel, we might start paying disproportionate attention to our posture and pain and the size of the callouses we surely must be growing on our knees (the lesser contemplatives' lesser stigmata), or just keeping our balance (another performance). If we stand, the same problems. If we lie down, other problems, the most obvious of which is falling asleep. Sitting is good because it is so simple and so hard. Again, the symbolism of the body is not insignificant. Sitting is the body language of passivity and receptivity. It is the stance easiest to maintain for a long period of time without necessary adjustment.

Finally, to pray we need to *shut up*. This is the prayer of silence we are talking about, and the silence must be serious. The first thing that must go is external noise, which includes music. Again, however efficient we might think it, combining music appreciation with prayer is detrimental to both. It is relatively easy to eliminate outside noise—at least those we can control. The harder part about shutting up is eliminating the internal noise. The first step, of course, is not speaking out loud. Then, we must try to let go the tightly controlled verbal processes inside our head, stop talking in sentences up there, and simply let go. Why? Because, once more, our language is a controlling mechanism. We may have stopped wheeling and dealing, may have sat down, but with our sentences we can continue our project in lively fashion.

How do we let go of our sentences? This is difficult, and precisely the point where many meditative techniques focus. What they agree on is that we need to *disengage* at one level and *engage* at another. We disengage from our internal monologue, and engage—whatever point or center or image or cloud of unknowing or third eye we have available. For some, the repetition of a phrase or mantra enables the disengagement; in the Christian tradition, the "Jesus Prayer" has had this function for many: "Lord Jesus Christ, have mercy on me a sinner." The point is not the meaning of the words, but their rhythmic repetition. Similarly, the rosary has been used as a means to silent contemplation. Anything can do, for the point is shutting

up the sort of language by which we constantly try to control our
lives and reality around us.

The Honesty of Silence.   What happens when we disengage from
our sentences? Do we enter into a world of placid serenity? Do we
hear God's Word? No, not as such. What we hear and see, rather
is all the stuff going on in our heads all the time without our knowing
it. When we disengage from *doing* verbally, we confront our internal
world of words and images and fantasies. And what a world it is!
We sit in silence, and around us whirl the projects we have formed,
the desires and cravings we feel, the angers and lusts, the "I should
have dones" and the "I should have saids" of past and planned
encounters. When we sit in silence, we see for the first time how
busy we are in our heads, how fearful, how compulsive. In a word,
we confront the truth about ourselves. We do not, in this sort of
silent prayer, ordinarily hear God's Word spoken to us. It does not
climax in a clear audition from the Other. What we most often
hear is our *own* word in all its jumbled, confused, self-aggrandizing
frenzy. It's pretty scary.

The prayer of silence is radical self-honesty before God. We allow
ourselves to glimpse the truth about ourselves, the way God sees
us all the time. The analogy that works best for me comes from
one of our children. When she and her siblings would leave their
beds at night and play (in disobedience to stern command) and
would be discovered, she would pull her nightgown up over her
head and continue blithely to play, thinking, "If I can't see them,
they can't see me." That, I think, expresses precisely our way of
living before God: "If I don't see myself, then God must not see
me either." The prayer of silence lifts the veil of self-deception, and
lays our hearts as open to ourselves as they are always to the God
who sees the mind and heart.

This is why the prayer of silence, however simple, is so terribly
difficult, and why almost all of us avoid it as much as we can.
Stopping is hard, sitting is boring, but silence is terrifying. Most of
us do not really want to know who we really are. But if we can stay
in the silence long enough, if we do not flee, then there is a sense
of presence in the emptiness. There does come a simple word—
"Yes." It is not a Word from God to us that gives us comfort. Rather
it is our word of faith, by which we say yes to this perception of
our self. It is the acceptance of the truth about ourselves as we are,
as in fact God sees us all the time. In the silence we come as close

as ever we do to the sense of utter otherness (for complete emptiness is close to total presence in the realm of the Spirit), come as close as we can to encountering our self as other; the prayer of silence in all its pain is grace, and a second word forms in our hearts, even amid the pain—"Thank you."

Prayer and Obedience. I need now to develop the third point about the prayer of silence, its function in the life of faith. I have suggested that it is the necessary precondition to the obedience of faith. To grasp this, we must remember how we are called and challenged by God through others in the world. We have our projects, dreams, desires, plans. We come up against the grace that is otherness. In otherness, we are addressed by God's Word. If we sin, we choose to ignore that Word, override it, continue our project as absolute. If we respond in faith, we take the other into account, say yes to the project of God that reveals itself in the multiple projects of others, allow our own project to be relativized, enter into the larger truth of God's world which is made up of others beside myself.

We do not directly hear God's Word in the prayer of silence, but our own word; and that is the entire point. We have seen earlier that the requirement of faith is *discernment*, what I have termed the asceticism of attentiveness or alertness. If we do not know what our own project is, how can we distinguish it from the projects we encounter in the world? If we do not know what *our* word is, how can we hear God's Word as it truly is? In prayer, we say yes to the truth about ourselves as idolaters, just as God says yes to us. By so doing, by entering into the presence/absence of God in silence, we *have already begun to relativize our project* by knowing it and identifying its idolatrous power. We are therefore able to hear and see the other *as other*, and not simply as a projection. We can tell the difference between our self and others, can therefore respond to the other without confusing the other with ourself. This is very simple, but essential. Without this distancing from our own project in silence, without relativizing it in the presence/absence of God, we will do one of two things, either submerge ourselves in the project of another without discrimination, or assimilate the other into our own project. I will consider in the next chapter these extremes of willfulness and will-lessness. For now it is necessary only to say that the antidote is found in the prayer of silence as the corollary of the obedience of faith.

The most obvious question about the prayer of silence is "how long must I stay in silence?" It would be easy to respond, "until it hurts," and there is some truth to that glib reply. One stays in silence for however long it takes for the "yes" of recognition to form, and with it the pain and shame of self-recognition, and following it, the word of thanks for this grace of truth. For those of us who never do it, each step must be more deliberate and awkward: stopping, sitting, shutting up. More time is required, because the process is not yet natural. The path of maturity moves in the direction of greater integration. As the process of silent self-honesty becomes habitual, it also becomes simpler. The oscillation between activity and silence is more rapid and flexible. In the finished Christian, the saint, one may not be able to detect extended periods of time alone, so rapid is the transition from silence to engagement with others, so constant. In the mature Christian, there does not appear the mechanical transition from solitude to society; as we shall see, the saint's freedom is characterized above all by availability. But it would be only another form of self-deception for those of us who have *not* gone through the arduous discipline of the prayer of silence to suppose that we were able to bypass its agonies. The criterion is not the prayer but its fruit: the obedience of faith to God in the structures of worldly existence, giving glory to God by the recognition of the Creator in every creature.

7

Faith Embodied:
Possessions and Power

The obedience of faith requires that we have a project of our own, as well as that we allow our project to be relativized by recognition of the Other. Humans are thereby placed in a state of constant tension, an oscillation between idolatry and faith. We are required by our constitution to close on every partial realization of truth; we are required by faith to open to every new offer of grace. Our freedom must navigate the tricky space between the joy of desire and the sorrow of deprivation.

Our constant temptation is to close once and for all, to stop the process that causes us pain even as it makes us grow. We seek to replace the risk of freedom with the security of compulsion, either in the direction of will-lessness or of willfulness. Neither is freedom; each is an escape from freedom. Each seeks to secure the self by eliminating the other. In will-lessness, I fail to form a project of my own. So great is my fear of deprivation that I refuse to desire. If I become a great pianist, I may be required to give it up. That would be too great a pain, so I never start taking piano lessons. In another form of will-lessness I simply adapt myself to someone else's project. I eliminate the tension between my project and the other by submerging myself in the other. Not only don't I want anything, whatever you want I will do. The delicate balance is equally destroyed by willfulness. Here, I eliminate otherness by submerging it in my project. I maintain the absoluteness of my desire and override any other's project with my own.

Models of spirituality can baptize will-lessness and willfulness in the name of faith. The gnostic model tends toward will-lessness. We do God's will by eliminating any desires of our own—indeed, by completely abandoning or denying our own desires, to do what is demanded of us by the other, any other. The liberation model tends toward willfulness. We know what God wants done, and it fits exactly with what we want done. Whether others desire it or not, we are going to do what is good for them. Both models miss the truth about faith: that freedom operates in the tension between closure and openness, and demands that everyone have a project.

These remarks may well appear abstract. I will try now to show how practical are their implications, by examining two aspects of our lives that involve our bodies: possessions and power. In effect, I am testing the model of spirituality I have sketched by returning it to the world of real people in society.

Before proceeding, however, it is good to remind ourselves just how slippery is this concept of world, and how the different models of spirituality define it. As I suggested in the introduction, the gnostic model tends to see the world as a problem, as a distraction to the spirit. Its physical reality and capacity to engage us destroys the divine within. The gnostic impulse therefore is to flee the world and construct an alternative society. In contrast, the liberation model rejoices in the physical reality of the world and is suspicious of talk about spirit in general. It sees the world in terms of oppressive social structures that prevent people from achieving their full personhood. But rather than flee the arena of human society, the liberation model seeks to transform it along the lines of its own vision of how humans should live.

The model of spirituality that I think is implied by the classic Christian creed locates itself somewhere between those extremes. First, insofar as the world is created by God at every moment, it is good. Second, insofar as the world can be shaped by idolatrous human projects and sin, it can also imprison and distort. Third, the meaning of the world is always subject to the disposition of human freedom and therefore also remains always ambiguous. Fourth, the proper human attitude toward the world is given by faith. This stance is best expressed by Paul: "I mean, brethren, the appointed time has grown very short; from now on, let those who have wives live as though they had none, and those who mourn as though they were not mourning, and those who rejoice as though they were not rejoicing, and those who buy as though they had no goods, *and those who deal with the world as though they had no dealings with it.* For the form of this world is passing away" (1 Cor. 7:29-31).

Paul's statement is remarkably dense. The issue he was addressing in 1 Corinthians 7 was whether people should marry or stay single in light of the expected end-time. But as so often, his words bear a significance of which he himself may not have been aware, and through which the Spirit speaks to the church. It is possible to read Paul's words faithfully apart from an immediate expectation of the end of all things, for as Paul himself surely understood it, the world is *always* passing away. The world is not a self-subsistent entity but one that comes into being and passes out of being by the will of its Creator. Every moment of the world's existence is by gift. Therefore the attitude Paul here encourages—some have called it a stance of "eschatological detachment"—is appropriate at every moment of our personal history or the history of the world.

What is this eschatological detachment? It derives immediately from what I have called obedient faith. Paul does not say that people should not marry or mourn or rejoice or buy or have dealings with the world. Indeed, his statement acknowledges that they *do* have such projects. Faith does not flee the world of human activity in will-lessness. It does not "go out of the world altogether" (1 Cor. 5:10). It engages the world. But it does so "as though not." The forming of human projects is not made absolute, and the world is not treated as though it were securely self-contained. Rather, every human project is relativized by the gift of God, which appears in the otherness of the world as it is created at every moment. Christian engagement of the world is therefore real but relative; it forms projects, but allows their intrinsic tendency toward absolutizing to be challenged. Above all, faith responds to the world as it now appears, as a fragile, relative, but real gift from God renewed constantly. And faith never forgets the deeply ambiguous character of the human project.

The Use of Possessions

What connection should there be between our Christian identity and our use of possessions? Here is a topic in which our appreciation for ambiguity is truly tested. Serious reflection on the Christian use of possessions must begin with the ambiguity both of our language about possessions (the slipperiness and inevitable relativity built into words such as rich and poor) and of our experience of possessions. We will not get far if we persist in thinking about possessions as a problem in the sense that a broken radio is a problem, so that if we could arrange all the pieces properly, everything would be solved. When we think about possessions, we are not in the realm of the problematic but in the realm of mystery. We are thinking about matters in which we are inextricably involved and from which we cannot distance ourselves without distortion. Possessions are an inevitable component of our existence as bodily creatures.

We must begin therefore with a realistic appreciation of our bodily condition, recognizing that we both have and are bodies. We *have* bodies in so far as we can dispose of them. But we *are* bodies in the sense that when we dispose of them we also dispose of our selves. This means that our bodies are the symbols of our selves. As we dispose of our bodies, so we signal our self-disposition in the world, not only to others but also to ourselves.

Not surprisingly, our project of becoming a person often involves considerable confusion between being and having. When we see how what we have (the things we touch and use) extends our bodies into the world, we can easily identify possessions with being. We want to stake claims over other things and other bodies, thinking that this will make us be more. The logic of somatic symbolism runs this way: more having equals more being. Seeing our things we see more of our selves, and so can others; we can measure our worth, and so can others. We cannot escape this ambiguity except by escaping our bodies altogether, a trick not available to us in this life.

Even if we could escape our bodily possessions, we could not rid ourselves of all the other things over which we can claim control as ours and see as measurements of our being and worth: our time, our space, our ideas, our imagination, even our virtue or sanctity. We can cling as tightly to those spiritual possessions as to stocks and bonds. The mystery of acquisitiveness is as powerful and as destructive in spiritual as in the physical realms.

When we look beyond our own bodies, we see that everyone around us is caught in the same tangle of being and having. All around us are disparities of having which are translated into disparities of being and worth. All around us is the same jingle-jangle of counting and measuring that we know so well from our private computations. We all calculate with one eye on ourselves and with one eye on the competition: who has the largest pile? Around us and within us flows the fascinating measurement of possessions and thereby of personal value: in terms of money, beauty, youth, brains, followers, friends, lovers, facelifts, jogging shoes, virtues. Is it any wonder, when we extend all this to the limitless reaches of world economic interdependence, with cartels and multinational corporations and colonial investment and computer-fed and generated stock crises, that we despair of ever getting this aspect of our lives into any coherent connection with our Christian identity and calling?

Few committed Christians are seriously tempted by the gross idolatry that makes possessions an end in themselves. The obsessive acquisitiveness of a Howard Hughes and the compulsive consumption of a Donald Trump are fascinating precisely because they are grotesque. There is today, unfortunately, a widely pervasive distortion of Christian perceptions concerning possessions, which deserves equal contempt. I refer to the "donate to the church and God will make you prosperous" theme of televangelism and God in Business organizations. This is clearly nothing more than a form of paganism, a perversion of the spirit of the beatitudes. One can only wonder at the wide and uncritical acceptance of this perversion by people who claim to take the New Testament seriously. In contrast to this subchristian phenomenon, the gnostic and liberation models of spirituality at least offer a way of dealing with possessions that can claim some coherent connection to the New Testament.

Gnostics and Liberationists. The gnostic model tends toward will-lessness. Christians within this model refuse any project with regard to possessions. They identify perfection with radical, evangelical poverty. In this they have the comfort of simplicity, and the biblical warrant of Jesus demanding of disciples that they leave all to follow him (Luke 14:33). Best of all, the monk or mendicant never has to consider the matter of possessions again; once the vow is made, there is no more ambiguity. So long as they maintain their distance from ownership, they are poor and perfect.

This option appears to be a simple closure, but it is not without ambiguities. Monks must face the odd consequence of their efficiency and community commitment, which is that they can claim to be poor only within increasingly prosperous communities. Mendicants must recognize the paradox that their radical life-style is enabled only by the financial support of those less perfect. The will-less option forgets, furthermore, that because of our bodily existence, we cannot ever cease being possessors altogether. Material things are only the most obvious symbols of human acquisitiveness; abandoning ownership of things by no means assures generosity in the sharing of nonmaterial possessions. Alas, the opposite often seems to be the case: without an obvious pile of things by which to measure our worth, we turn to intangibles with an equally greedy eye. Most of all, the gnostic option concerns itself only with the perfection of the individual. It forgets that the obedience of faith demands a poverty far more rigorous, a self-emptying far more continuous, than that accomplished once for all by a vow.

Repelled by the privatism implicit in the gnostic attitude toward possessions, other Christians follow the lead of the liberation model, which sees the perfect fulfillment of the gospel in the equalization of possessions. This model can look to the idealized presentation of the first community in Jerusalem, which was of one heart and soul and shared all its possessions in common, no one calling anything his or her own (Acts 4:32-37). Thus they work for the structural change of economic systems, the divestiture of the oppressive rich and the emancipation of the oppressed poor. They dream of a classless society in which the goods of the earth will be shared by all, and their passion and energy is directed to the task of "doing justice on the earth."

No project could appear more simple or clear-cut. But the very feature that is its greatest attraction is also the source of its problems. It reduces the complexity inherent in possessions to a matter of economic processes. If radical poverty forgets the inevitable demands of the body, the quest for a utopian communism forgets that possessiveness is rooted in the passions of the human heart, the idolatrous impulse of self-aggrandizement. We may cut our material pie equally, but by so doing, we simply displace the competitive urge and the compulsion to measure worth by having to other endeavors, for example to the contest for power. An imposed structural equality demands as well a rigid social control and—inevitably, once we are in an arena larger than a small voluntary group—the totalitarian rule required to exercise that control.

There is also the problem that the biblical basis for an economically egalitarian society is slender, selective, and suspect. The vision owes far more to Plato than to the Prophets. Above all, the liberation model is a perfect example of willfulness. It leaps right into God's project and makes it our own. It assumes that we know exactly what the kingdom of God is supposed to look like, and that we even have a blueprint. It assumes, therefore, that we not only know the mind of God but that we know how to mirror God's will adequately in the concrete structures of society. This is arrogant enough—far more than the gnostic model, which never claims more than the perfection of the individual, after all—but what is worse, this leap into the divine project suggests disingenuously that *we* ourselves have no project concerning possessions, but are only engaged in God's work.

Like the monk who supposes that making a vow and living in a community of possessions relieves him of ever having to think about possessions again (and thus closes the obedience of faith), so the liberationist might suppose that by working for the perfect form of society, he too has bypassed the problem of possessions in his own life (thus closing the obedience of faith). Both are wrong, and for the same reason: obedient faith demands of us the forming of a project concerning possessions, but it also demands a constant willingness to change that project in the light of new experience.

The Teaching of Paul.   The way possessions function within the obedience of faith is shown most clearly by Paul. We have seen already that Paul's statement concerning eschatological detachment in 1 Cor. 7:30-31 included, "let those who buy act as though they had no goods, and those who deal with the world as though they had no dealings with it." In the use of possessions, Paul calls for the attitude of "as though not." This means, first, that he does not call for a radical material dispossession as a criterion for Christian membership; Paul nowhere demands poverty as a corollary of faith. Indeed, he praises the positive use of possessions to provide hospitality for missionaries (see Philem. 4-7; Phil. 4:14-18). But neither does Paul demand a community of possessions. Christians are neither to flee the world nor to construct alternative social structures, and for the same reason: their identity and call always and everywhere transcend both options: the form of this world is *always* passing away. Paul sees that Christians continue to buy and sell in the world. He himself works at a trade, and expects his converts to do likewise (see 1 Thess. 4:11; 2 Thess. 3:6-13). And although he himself does not make use of it, he insists that ministers of the Gospel have a right to be financially supported by their communities (1 Cor. 9:3-14).

Paul's most extended discussion of possessions involves the great
fund-raising project he directed for the Jerusalem church (2 Cor.
8–9). He had agreed to undertake this money-raising venture early
in his ministry, "to remember the saints" of that city (Gal. 2:10),
whose attempt at communal possessions was short-lived or unsuc-
cessful. As Paul's success in converting Gentiles increased, the need
for the collection grew greater, since his mission generated resent-
ment among fellow Jews. Sensitive to the symbolic potential inherent
in possessions, Paul saw the collection taken up among his congregations as a gesture of reconciliation between Gentile and Jewish
Christians.

In his first letter to the Corinthians, Paul sets up the procedures
for the collection (1 Cor. 16:1-4). It is obvious that the fund-raising
effort involves considerable planning and coordination between communities. In 2 Corinthians, he writes at a time when the success of
the enterprise is in doubt at least partly because the Corinthian
congregation, suspicious of Paul on several counts (11:9; 12:14-19),
is not cooperating in the effort (9:1-5). In his attempt to encourage
participation, Paul shares his perceptions concerning possessions.
He sees the sharing of material possessions as a kind of mutual gift-
giving: the Jerusalem church had shared the spiritual blessings of
the good news with the Gentiles; it is therefore appropriate now
for the Gentiles to respond with material assistance (2 Cor. 8:14;
see Rom. 15:27). Possessions, we see, symbolize relationships. We
notice as well that the kind of sharing required is to be determined
by the discernment of need: at this moment it might be a spiritual
gift, at another moment, a material gift.

Paul uses the term "equality" in his discussion, but it is clear that
he does not mean a structural levelling; rather, he interprets equality
to mean "reciprocity" (2 Cor. 8:14). Sharing of possessions may
cause hardship and even impoverishment for some at the material
level (8:2-3). What makes this acceptable is not their desire to be
unfettered by materiality, or the goal of creating of a utopian society,
but only *the needs of others* (8:12-15). Paul therefore sees the sharing
of possessions as an articulation of obedient faith, requiring the
same sort of discernment as all faith demands. It is a matter, he
says, of "obedience to the Gospel" (9:13), and also of thanksgiving
to God (9:12), for God is the giver of all good gifts, and the good
news is precisely the message concerning the gift that God has
shared first with us (9:14-15).

Paul thinks it perfectly appropriate for individual Christians and communities to shape their own projects with regard to possessions. They are free to do business (1 Cor. 7:30) and have a trade (1 Thess. 4:3), to support their own households financially (1 Tim. 5:4, 16), to support their leaders and teachers (Gal. 6:6; 1 Cor. 9:14; 1 Tim. 5:17), to run community welfare programs for orphans and widows (1 Tim. 5:3-16). These are legitimate projects, and can vigorously be pursued. The response of obedient faith comes into play when these legitimate projects are challenged by the needs of others. Now, individuals and communities must respond to a call other than that of their own self-interest, security, or even survival. In Paul's situation, the call was put by the physical needs of the Jerusalem churches, and the overarching spiritual need to establish harmony between all the churches of God. In this context, Paul calls his communities to relativize their private and even their communal projects, in order to make their possessions (money, time, energy, space, concern) available to others, even if this comes at considerable cost to themselves.

The mature Christian use of possessions is therefore an articulation of the obedience of faith. It respects the implications of bodily existence and the inevitable social context of life before God. It recognizes that humans must form projects of their own concerning possessions, and that these are kept from becoming absolute by the challenge presented by the needs of others. The sharing of possessions is demanded by faith, not to demonstrate the perfection of the individual or as an exercise in social engineering, but as a response to the project of God in the world as revealed in the physical and spiritual needs of our neighbors. Paul characteristically gives as the greatest motivation for this sharing the messianic pattern found in what we have learned to call "the mind of Christ": "You know the grace of our Lord Jesus Christ, that though he was rich, yet for your sake he became poor, so that by his poverty you might become rich" (2 Cor. 8:9).

The Gospels and Jesus.   If we look to the Gospels to find specific directions on possessions we shall find ourselves confused, not by the lack of commands but by their multiplicity and diversity. If we scan only the Gospel of Luke, which gives most explicit attention to the issue, we find that the poor are blessed (6:20) and the rich are cursed (6:24). Consistent with this, disciples are to leave all their possessions to follow Jesus (14:33). But on the other hand, followers of Jesus are to give alms (12:33; 16:1-13) and provide hospitality (10:38-42). The commands are not capable of simultaneous fulfillment. In Acts, likewise, the ideal of giving up ownership and holding all possessions in common (4:32-35) stands in tension with the far more persistent ideal of almsgiving (9:36; 10:2; 11:27-30).

We do better to look to Jesus and see how the poverty that is the obedience of faith is enacted. Jesus' poverty did not consist in his giving up material possessions; he and his followers were supported by others (Luke 8:1-3) and from their purse they could give alms (John 13:29). His poverty was his refusal to identify his life in what he had but "in every word that comes from the mouth of God" (Matt. 4:4). He did not "reckon equality with God something to be seized" but emptied himself out in obedience to his Father moment by moment in the circumstances of his life (Phil. 2:6-11). When he would preach, he was called to heal (Mark 1:37-45); when he would rest he was called to teach (6:31-34); when he would teach he was called to feed (6:35-44); when he would live he was called to die (14:33-36). By such poverty even unto death, did he enrich us with the power of new life.

The Exercise of Power

We begin with the recognition of the real but relative power that we have (on loan), and are (by gift), simply by virtue of our existence. We exercise power simply by *being*. Power is rooted first of all in our bodily presence. Everything physical displaces some space, and by so doing exerts at a minimum the passive power of resistance. Every physical thing, therefore, must be taken into account. A chair placed between me and the exit may not appear to exercise power. But if I wish to see the door whole, I must move the chair. To get to the door, I must go around the chair. A mountain obviously exerts a dramatically greater power. It may keep me prisoner in this valley. It may require the risk of my life to get beyond it.

As in the case of possessions, our psychosomatic synergism as humans increases the potential as well as the puzzling character of our personal power. Our power is increased because we are far more than inert matter. We move and dispose of ourselves. You can choose to play the role of the chair between me and the exit. Many of us can join hands and make a mountain impossible to get around. And because our physical disposition depends on the subjectivity of spirit, I can extend my power into the realm of others' freedom as well. We get inside each other's bodies by the leap of the spirit in knowledge and love. As you sit and read this book, your mind and body are to some extent oriented by my mind and body. I am, willy-nilly, exercising a great deal of power in our author-reader relationship. From another perspective, you the reader exercise greater power over me the author. By holding the book and by reading it, you enable me to speak. By tossing the book aside, you cast a deciding vote!

Personal power is therefore not intelligible in isolation but only in a relational context. If nobody wants to leave the room, that troublesome chair's power to block egress is fairly meaningless. But if a fire breaks out in this crowded room, and everybody needs to leave the room at once, the chair's power becomes lethal. If I have no need to cross into the next valley, the mountain's presence is only suggestive and scenic. If I need to find a lost climber, the mountain's power becomes active and fearful. The exercise of power must also be placed in the context of the human community, in the exchange of bodies and minds that is society. In a word, personal power is inevitably political; its exercise always impinges on the common life of humans.

Few serious Christians are tempted, I think, by blatantly idolatrous projects involving power. They find a Stalin or Idi Amin no more appealing than they do plutocrats. Most observers, in fact, have been able to recognize in the genocidal cruelty of this century a qualitative difference from the tyrannies of the past. Where once some constraint was placed on pope and czar and king by tradition or conscience, the totalitarian urge today recognizes no restraint. Recognizing the bloated cruelty of power fanatically wielded in the name of abstract truth, most Christians have also rejected the church's own dismal record of structural violence through inquisition and statecraft. But now it seems even more difficult to place power within the context of sanctity. The tension proper to authentic faith is easily lost between the extremes of will-lessness and willfulness.

Will-lessness. The will-less option refuses to have a project of power. Acknowledging my power is as frightening as acknowledging the presence of my body. Perfection must consist in cutting away this presence, removing myself from the ambiguity of the body. If I do not acknowledge the power that is mine, I can also refuse to use it. I stay out of politics of any sort because it always involves compromise and debate in the attempt to influence others. How could I possibly be certain of the purity of my intention or action? I may abuse power or end up with dirty hands associated with the corrupt uses of power.

For the sake of simplicity and security in my sanctity, I act as though I were powerless. For fear of influencing your mind, I will write a bad book, or give a poor lecture. For fear of damaging your career, I will give you a good grade on a bad paper, or refuse to give grades at all. Lest I interfere with my spouse's liberty, I will not object to his adulterous absences or abusive presence. I refuse to acknowledge the power I have already exercised and that is mine because I have given birth to children, so I refuse to shape their minds or correct their infantile impulses, allowing them to form bizarre projects of their own. In short, I create a power vacuum, and allow anyone who wants more power to take it. I remove myself from the conversation. This can be expressed spatially by becoming a hermit, clinically by withdrawal in depression.

But what is the consequence of my fearful refusal to form my own project of power? The result is that in the absence of my project other people's projects become distorted and distended. My children grow into monsters of narcissism because they never confront me as parent. My husband becomes a bully because my power never checks his own. The chairman becomes a petty tyrant because the board allows him to swell like a toad in their tiny corporate pond. The leader becomes tyrant when hers is the only voice in the land. Idolatry is enabled by the absence of otherness.

Just as the powerful presence of others is necessary for me to have the obedience of faith, so must I be powerful for others to respond in faith. God speaks to me through the many voices of others. In exactly the same way, *my* voice is necessary for God to speak to others. If I refuse to form a project, if I am will-less, then that part of God's voice is silent in the world. If I have no project, then I remove from the others in my world the possibility of growing in faith. They are allowed by my withdrawal to remain in their idolatry. I must be powerful in order for others to be faithful, because I must be other for them to be graced.

Willfulness.   The other extreme concerning power is willfulness. This is manifested by the liberation model, which seeks the kingdom of God in the reshaping of the social order. But it is found equally in the contemporary conservative movements sometimes called "fundamentalist" Christianity. Fundamentalism appears on the sur-face to be the exact opposite of liberationism, since it is right-wing in its politics and liberation movements are always left-wing. Al-though their visions of what a reshaped society is have little in common, nevertheless, they actually share many of the same pre-suppositions, particularly the one that society as a whole must reflect a certain truth in its structures.

Considered by itself, of course, this is simply the legitimate practice of politics. The liberationist (or fundamentalist) approach to power becomes willful, however, when it seeks to bypass politics and—more critically, for us—bypasses the dynamics of the obe-dience of faith, which require that the projects of others be taken into account, and that we maintain an openness to what God is saying in the multiplicity of other voices in the world. Willfulness reveals itself in two moments. The first is the decision that we have the total truth concerning the proper ordering of society and need listen to no other voices. This is the essential mark of ideology, which distinguishes it from a theology that articulates the obedience of faith. No debate is necessary, no further data need be considered; we know what is right, and all that remains is to do it. When ideology is the starting point, all ambiguity is removed, for all "otherness" is eliminated. The second aspect of willfulness is the readiness to impose on others what we understand to be God's project, whether they want it or not.

The frightening aspect of this approach is its edge of fanaticism, a distortion of faith all the more dangerous because it counterfeits something essential and true—in this case, the legitimacy of a project of power. When we assume we know God's will and have an obligation to carry it out, we have begun to absolutize our own project of power in the name of God. Operating in the name of God, and alienated from our own agenda, we can legitimate force and even violence for the sake of the kingdom of God. I can destroy the property of those who practice abortion. I can threaten the lives of those who carry weapons. I can steal from those who steal. I can carry on a bloody war of revolution for the sake of the poor who themselves perhaps show little interest in such revolution. I can discriminate and show hatred toward those who have hated and discriminated against us. I can oppress those who have oppressed us. And all in the name of Jesus!

I find two basic problems in such radical movements—and, I repeat, they come from the "right" as much as from the "left." First, that they use Christian rhetoric to camouflage a project of power that in its absolutizing instinct is contrary to the gospel and obedient faith. Second, they accept the totalitarian equation of Lenin, this century's prototypical social engineer, that the ordinary processes of politics are insufficient to bring about a more just social order, and that violence is not only the legitimate but the appropriate exercise of power. By no means do I mean to imply that heroism and even self-sacrifice may not be demanded of us in the face of palpable and obvious evil. But even in such circumstances, the norms of "the mind of Christ" must apply.

It is important to point out that will-lessness and willfulness both distort the authentic response of faith and, paradoxically, lead to the same result. When we refuse to exercise the power that is ours in virtue of our existence, then we allow the projects of others to swell grotesquely and invite the force and violence we suffer. Power refused makes force necessary later; force refused leads to violence.

The Acceptance of Power.   The mature exercise of power begins with the acceptance of it as part of the gift of creation, and with the willingness to form a legitimate human project. It is appropriate to seek to use my mind and body to accomplish certain goals. It is right for communities and societies to propose and plan for the betterment of the group, the establishment of justice, the cultivation of peace. It is necessary to work with others for purposes of persuasion and change. At the same time, we recognize the inevitable ambiguity of all such power. Rooted in the messy complexity of bodies and communities, it can never be totally pure. But this need not paralyze us, for we know as well that our power is partial, not total. So long as I live with other humans, my project will confront and be relativized by the projects of other free subjects. And our shared project is relativized by the project of God working through us all. The project of God (which is never ours as a possession and never known by us except after the fact) is worked out precisely in this interplay of human projects.

My acceptance of power means also an appreciation that I am only one body. It is therefore all the more important to decide where and when to place this body. Herein is the risk of faith. I cannot be in two places at once. If I walk the picket line, I cannot be at the park with my daughter, or lecturing to my class, or writing this book, or visiting the sick. And if I place my body with my daughter at the duck pond, I cannot march in the anti-nuclear rally. Thus the risk. I cannot know which of these projects is most right or most urgent; I cannot calculate the consequences of my absence or presence. The first task of the life of faith, therefore, is to form good and honest projects, using my real but relative power in the way I can see best at the moment, trusting the living God who knows my heart to judge me, and trusting God to break in and challenge this project when needful. I must pay attention to my daughter, keep an eye on the duck pond, but also keep listening.

This understanding of power includes awareness of its contextual character. It is in company with others that my project is given approbation but also called into question. And this is what bothers us. Most of us would prefer a perfection to be somewhere near our navel or in the headlines. We would like to have a power that is in our total possession (self-control) or one that governs all the world (cosmic control). We dislike the messy give and take of many projects in the community. We complain about its inefficiency for the doing of good; we fail to appreciate that its complexity also prevents the doing of even greater evil. We think of compromise as a failure, rather than as an articulation of faith by which we commit together (co-promise) a use of power for the common good rather than for our own self-aggrandizement. Despite our nods to participatory democracy, we detest dialogue. We hate debate and discernment and decision making together. But this, I insist, is where God's project for the world is given expression: in the messy conversation between many voices, in the genuine give and take of multiple perspectives and plans and projects, in the listening and discerning and obedience of faith, in reciprocity and exchange.

Paul and Jesus.   Such was the understanding of power held by Paul, who saw it most perfectly expressed in what he termed weakness. Paul did not think of this weakness as the failure to have a project; it did not mean lack of desire or will. Rather, it meant the willingness to expose the self and one's desires and above all one's physical presence to others, even when they were hostile, thus making oneself vulnerable to them. The extravagant way in which Paul did this with his communities is vividly etched in his letters, above all in his second letter to the Corinthians. Even as he acknowledges his foolishness in making so blatant his desires and hopes for the community's acceptance of him, he continues to do so (2 Cor. 11–12). Paul did not withhold himself from his churches in aloofness or disdain, did not stand on his rights (power) as an apostle. He used every means of rhetoric and discipline available to persuade them of his project. This, he knew, was seen by them as weakness rather than as power. But Paul was convinced that such was the way God's power was at work in the world, through the paradoxical weakness of bodily presence, in the cross of Jesus (2 Cor. 13:4).

In Jesus, the power of God was manifested through the body language of service, the disposal of his body for others. The project of God as revealed in the faith of Jesus was not one of withdrawal from the crowd for the sake of personal enlightenment and self-control unstained by the messiness of politics and sinners. Nor was God's project revealed in the organized attempt to overthrow the military and economic oppressors of the empire. It was revealed in Jesus' physical presence at meals with sinners and tax collectors (petty politicians, after all). It was shown in his touching of lepers and restoring them to human community; in his speaking to women and recognizing their humanity—no matter if husbanded or not; in his holding little children in his arms, for the kingdom is all about the marginal and useless; in his feeding the multitude and meeting their need for food so that they could have the strength for higher education; in his going to the tombs, confronting the possessed, and—after healing them—sitting with them, talking; in his walking on dusty roads with unsophisticated fishermen; in his having friends among women and men in villages; in his telling little stories of seeds and sheep and coins and lost children concerning God's kingdom; in his going into the assemblies of his opponents and speaking with them and hearing their attacks and not flinching; in his anger at stupidity and arrogance and evil; in his weeping at a friend's death; in his sweeping coins off the tables of the bankers in the temple and kicking over their stands and flailing a whip at them; in his breaking bread and sharing wine, in his stretching out of his arms.

This is how Jesus summarized the power of the presence of God's rule in himself: "The Son of Man came also not to be served but to serve, and to give his life as a ransom for many" (Mark 10:45); and, even more simply: "I am among you as one who serves" (Luke 22:27). Paul put it this way, "Christ did not please himself; but, as it is written, 'The reproaches of those who reproached thee fell on me'" (Rom. 15:3). Such foolishness. Such weakness. But for Paul, this messianic pattern is precisely the way in which "God was in Christ reconciling the world to himself" (2 Cor. 5:19). The cross was "the power of God and the wisdom of God; for the foolishness of God is wiser than humans, and the weakness of God is more powerful than humans" (1 Cor. 1:25).

For Paul, therefore, the pattern of Jesus' self-disposition became the paradigm for his own work with his communities. Paul's apostolic authority was not exercised by absolute removal from the crowd or by absolute control of the crowd. It was played out in the risky, day-by-day, relative and relational, embarrassing and complicated power of personal presence and persuasion, in which (he was convinced), God's power also was at work: "He . . . is powerful in you. For he was crucified in weakness, but lives by the power of God. For we are weak in him, but in dealing with you we shall live with him by the power of God" (2 Cor. 13:3-4).

8

Doing the Truth in Love:
Anger and Sexuality

*C*hristians who rarely can agree on anything else agree that the
commandment "love your neighbor as yourself" (Lev. 19:18),
expresses the central obligation toward each other that faith in God
demands of us. Jesus identified it, together with "love for God," as
the central commandment of Torah (Mark 12:30-31; Matt. 22:37-
39; Luke 10:27); and he makes it the attitude distinctive to his
community: "This I command you, to love one another" (John
15:17). Paul says love sums up all the law, "because it does no harm
to a neighbor" (Rom. 13:9-10); James designates it the "law of the
Kingdom" (James 2:8); Peter demands of his readers "unfailing love
for one another since love covers a multitude of sins"; and John
concurs: "This commandment we have from him, that he who loves
God should love his brother also" (1 John 4:21). Paul, as we have
seen, makes *agape* the one gift that endures, and the "higher way"
that Christians should pursue (1 Cor. 12:31).

The Difficult Commandment

Assenting to the command of love is far easier than carrying it out.
The love commandment has proven to be a tough assignment. It
presents us immediately with the problem inherent in all positive
commands, which is their open-endedness. If the child as she leaves

the house is told by her mother, "Do not cross the street or climb the tree," the little girl remains free to do whatever else she chooses within those broad restrictions. But if the mother tells the girl, "Go out and have fun," the child is far more constrained. Positive commands tend toward perfectionism. They do not make clear when what is commanded has been fulfilled.

Another difficulty in keeping Jesus' love commandment lies in understanding its terms. Who is my neighbor, after all, and what does it mean to love the neighbor as myself? These criteria can grow terribly complex. If I declare that whomever I next encounter is my neighbor (and there is certainly some truth to that position), then in the real world where I encounter many others, I am forced to discern the competing claims of loyalty placed on me: does the derelict whom I do not know but who is obviously in great need have claim on my attention and possessions equal to or surpassing that of my wife or daughter?

How is self-love an appropriate criterion for loving others? What kind or degree of self-love is appropriate as the measure or perhaps even the condition for love of the neighbor? The difficulty is compounded by the variations in the commandment proposed by the New Testament itself. Thus, in Jesus' parable of the Good Samaritan, told precisely as an interpretation of this commandment, the point is not "who is my neighbor" but "to whom can I show myself as neighbor?" The issue gets turned around from the object of love to the subject who is loving. Even more difficult, the Gospel of John puts the command not in terms of loving the neighbor as we love our selves, but rather: "This is my commandment, that you love one another as I have loved you" (John 15:12). The love of God shown to us in the Messiah becomes the measure of our love for each other. Once more we are invited to look to Jesus (Heb. 12:3) or to the messianic norm (Gal. 6:2), now in terms of the way Jesus disposed himself for others, the Son of God "who loved me and gave himself for me" (Gal. 2:20).

A final difficulty in understanding, much less performing, the commandment of loving the neighbor is the term love itself. Simple enough, perhaps, to make the obvious (and appropriate) semantic distinctions between the Greek word *agapē* uniformly used in the New Testament for this attitude, and other kinds of love expressed by the terms *eros* or *philia*. If *eros* is fundamentally the movement of love that seeks unity with the other because the other is desirable, and *philia* is the love of friendship which seeks fellowship with the other because of shared interests and perceptions, then *agapē* is to will the good of the other simply for the other's sake.

But that is not quite right, either. *Agapē* does not do what the other wants simply because the other wants it, but wills what is truly good for the other. But this raises the issue how we can tell what is good for the other. In Eph. 4:15, Paul exhorts his readers to "do the truth in love." It is an extraordinary expression even in its formulation: Paul makes "truthing" a verb, so that "doing truth" and "love" are mutually interpretive terms. The statement is noteworthy also because in context, it clearly refers not only to "speaking truth" (as the RSV has it), although that is the immediate contrast intended to the "deceitful wiles" of others; rather, by "doing the truth in love" Paul means the mode by which the community as community "grows into maturity" as the body of Christ (4:15-16). In effect, Christian love must be measured by the truth, and truth in relationships must be measured by love.

This in fact was the reason I listed *agapē* as a dimension of *faith* in an earlier discussion. It is faith that properly aligns the human project to the world and its Creator, and therefore as well to all other creatures. It is the perception of faith that acknowledges the other as other, answerable solely to the Other who is Creator, rather than to me and my project. Only in faith can I seek the other's good in the fullest sense, as a creature known and loved by God. This is the dimension of "truth" that governs Christian *agapē*.

By no means does it thereby become easy to exercise *agapē* in truth. All the difficulties of discernment inherent in every response of obedient faith accompany as well every response of love for the neighbor. We can never know in the act whether we are truly seeking the other's good or simply imposing our own project, whether we are acting willfully or will-lessly. Loving in truth is also filled with risk and pain, as well as the unanticipated joy of growth in the Spirit of God. Nor can we ever consistently and with absolute finality sort out those idealized semantic distinctions between *eros*, *philia*, and *agapē*. As bodily and emotional creatures, our freedom is conditioned by elements of desire and longing even as we seek the good of the other.

In the present chapter, I will address two aspects of "doing the truth in love" that are particularly problematic for the spiritual life because they so intensely involve the somatic, psychic and social dimensions of our existence. I will consider in turn the connection between anger and *agapē*, and between sexuality and *agapē*.

Anger: The Hardest Virtue

Anger is not obviously an expression of love. Still less is it part of the classical understanding of the spiritual life. We associate anger with distasteful feelings and disastrous situations. So also did the ancient Greek moralists who excoriated anger as inappropriate to the sage. The virtuous person was marked by *apatheia*, and no emotion was so manifestly rude and disruptive as anger. At first reading, the New Testament appears to endorse the view that anger is incompatible with *agapē*. James tells us to be slow to speech and slow to anger, "for human anger does not work the righteousness of God" (James 1:19-20). Paul also tells us to put away anger as a characteristic of the "old self" that we no longer are (Col. 3:8; Eph. 4:26). He tells his communities to pray with uplifted hands "apart from all anger" (1 Tim. 2:8). Paul and James here seem to be in direct continuity with the mind of Jesus, who appears decisively to forbid any anger in his radical interpretation of the commandment, "Thou shalt not kill." Jesus says, "I say to you that every one who is angry with his brother shall be liable to judgment; whoever insults his brother shall be liable to the council, and whoever says, 'You fool!' shall be liable to the hell of fire" (Matt. 5:22).

Jesus gave us many other commandments that we have not taken nearly so seriously. In the same sermon he told us "Do not swear at all" (Matt. 5:34) and "Do not resist one who is evil" (5:39). Christians have never taken those commands with the same seriousness as they have the prohibitions of lust and anger, which tells us less about our commitment to Jesus' words than about the parts of our own lives we find hardest to manage. In any case, the prohibition of anger is pervasive in Christian spirituality. Anger is considered virtually the opposite of true spirituality. The saint is supposed to be impassive, imperturbable, self-controlled, incapable of anger. Many of us have grown up thinking of anger and love as mutually exclusive; "Don't be angry," we were told, "be charitable."

All of this is wrong, an error distorting human life, a lie begetting other lies. The error stems from a misapprehension concerning anger itself and for that reason a misunderstanding of the New Testament prohibitions of anger, including that issued by Jesus. Most of all, it misreads the story of Jesus, whose footsteps in faith we are called to follow.

Rectification of the error begins with a clearer perception of anger. We must distinguish between a human emotion and an attitude.

Emotions are rooted in our psychosomatic makeup; they are the natural, inevitable products of our bodies. Attitudes, in contrast, are dispositions of our freedom; they involve choice. The distinction is of critical importance concerning anger, for anger properly defined is simply an emotion, rooted in our bodily being. Physiologically, anger is the rush of adrenalin through our systems to activate our bodies in a response to threat or danger. Anger is a defense and survival mechanism. Without anger we could not resist attack, or overcome obstacles.

Anger invariably occurs when an intended action is thwarted, or a present condition is threatened. If I am rushing to the door and a chair falls in my path, anger is a natural physiological response. If the chair should also happen to fall across my legs and cause me pain, then my anger is even more emphatic, for not just my project but my body is threatened. One might interject at this point, "Oh, but *that* isn't really *anger*. It's too small. Jesus could not be condemning that." I agree that Jesus was not condemning this emotional response, but I do argue that this *is* anger in the most proper sense. Anger at this level *is* small. It is not a towering rage. It is not hostility or hatred. It does not seek the destruction of the other. It is simply the charge of energy fueling a response to challenge. As such, it is simply a consequence of being a body in the world with other bodies, with whom we unavoidably conflict and collide. And as such it is part of the very constitution of our being as God has created and continues to create us.

Anger is also a corollary of obedient faith. Remember how we have defined faith: the human project is challenged by the call of God voiced by the projects of others in the world. Why anger? Because when I am asked to release control of my own project, my self-preoccupation, my private truth, I perceive it first as a threat to my very self. I instinctively try to resist the threat, to defend myself against the danger represented by the other. Faith is the obedience which must overcome the resistance to God's call that is our own idolatrous project. Therefore it inevitably generates anger. Anger at those whose needs call me out of a preoccupation with my own needs? Yes, of course. Anger at God, who calls me precisely through these projects which invite and prod me beyond my own? Most certainly.

As an emotion, then, anger is a sign of truth. It tells us the truth about our bodies and our souls in the world with others. It tells us (and others) what our projects are. It tells us and God what our idolatries are. The process is simple and direct: whatever causes me anger shows some project of mine being threatened. Anger is a marvelous diagnostician. But if it reveals the truth about ourselves to others, then it also renders us vulnerable to others. In our anger we reveal ourselves as we really are: what we care about, what frightens us, what loss causes us grief, what can hurt us.

When we show our anger, we are open to the gaze of others, and therefore to the possibility of being hurt again. To be angry with another, therefore, is an act of intimacy. To allow another to see my anger is an act of trust. As an emotion, anger speaks truth about ourselves and others. It is an instrument of love.

Will-lessness and Willfulness.　If what I have said is true, why is anger so problematic for the spiritual life? The difficulty comes not with anger as an emotion, but with the ways we express or fail to express it, the choices which turn into *attitudes*. We can choose to express anger simply and directly and appropriately as a revelation of our self, and when we do, anger does not harm. But other, more destructive choices are also available. Remember, if anger is intimacy and self-revelation, it is potentially dangerous to us and our projects. If others learn how to hurt us, they can do so again. To show grief at a loss is to invite further loss. And because anger as emotion rushes through our bodies, causing them to shake or to clench involuntarily, and leaving them limp, we do not feel in control when we are angry; indeed, we feel maximally exposed and vulnerable to the attacks of others. In short, accepting anger means once more accepting our fully human condition, our contingency, our real but relative power, our inevitable condition as possessors who can suffer loss. It is far safer for us to move with our anger in the direction of will-lessness or willfulness, either to deny the reality of anger, or turn it into God's project.

The will-less option seeks to deny anger altogether. As with possessions and power, the denial gains us some safety and control, but at considerable cost to our humanity and to doing the truth in love. With anger, indeed, the cost is even more severe, because the energy generated by anger does not simply disappear when we dismiss it. If anger is not openly and appropriately expressed, it tends to build within us, creating an internal pressure. The more it gathers within, of course, the more frightening its potency appears. Now, even greater psychic energy is required to keep *it* under control. At its logical extreme the body language of such control is catatonia.

My anger is so great that I cannot move at all, lest I destroy the world. If I even began to express this rage, I think, I would kill.

When our attempts at repression of anger are successful, the result is emotional withdrawal and coldness. We reach that state of apathy we associate with the stereotypical and thoroughly unattractive "perfect" person who is at once completely in control and completely unspontaneous. The cost of such stoic *apatheia* is the surgical removal of desire. We must expend all our energy holding back our anger within; we have none left over to deal with challenge from without. Therefore, we present a mask of impassivity to the world.

More often, the amputation is less than total. Our diseased and distorted anger seeps into the atmosphere around us, poisoning and perverting our relations with others, without our even being conscious of it. We are all familiar with the repressed anger underlying activities such as teasing. We have come to recognize the massive resistance organized by the attitudes we call passive-aggressive. These are the forms of revenge our emotions take on us when we do not acknowledge them or allow them to live.

The willful option, in contrast, turns anger into a project. Anger is directed systematically at others designated as enemies. Our enemies are evil and we are righteous. Our fury can therefore safely, even nobly, be vented in their direction. The real but relative anger that enables me to respond to my immediate context is too frightening and, if revealed, makes me too vulnerable. But I can control the rage that I project onto an absolutized object. Such are the societal hostilities aimed at Gypsies or Jews or Communists or gays. The rage has nothing to do with specific persons or actions. It is a fury displaced from the real world of small plans and projects and frustrations onto the fantasy world of international conspiracies and cosmic conflicts. Hostility works in the service of those wishing to be the instruments of God's retributive justice. So the fundamentalist Moral Majority can indulge a burning rage against all the satanic perverters of morality. So liberationists can spew invective against the rich or the white or the males who personify in their imperialistic conspiracies the reign of evil in the world.

The will-less and willful distortions of anger turn it into a virulent force. When anger is not directed to its immediate, available, and appropriate targets from the beginning, it grows into an attitude of hostility. And it is *hostility*, not anger, that leads to the doing of murder. Murder is the fruit of anger denied and distorted. It is such hostility, I suggest, that Jesus condemned. When he called anger as bad as murder, he did not mean the *emotion* of anger, but the *attitude* of rage and hostility which leads to murder, just as when he called lust as bad as adultery, he did not mean involuntary sexual arousal, but the intention to seduce and conquer another sexually. Jesus did not condemn our physical beings as created by God, but the diseases of our freedom.

Paul and Jesus.   If we look again at the New Testament passages that condemn anger, we discover that it is precisely hostility that they reject. Thus Paul says in Eph. 4:31, "Let all bitterness and wrath and anger and clamor and slander be put away from you, with all malice." He does not condemn an emotional state, but attitudes and actions. In contrast, he says, "be kind to one another, tenderhearted, forgiving one another, as God in Christ forgave you" (4:32). If there is no anger as emotion, however, then there is no awareness of and acknowledgment of hurt or injury, and there can be no forgiveness. Anger is virtually a prerequisite of reconciliation, for it reveals the reality of estrangement. It is an emotion that tells the truth about our relationships. Paul therefore tells us a few lines earlier in Ephesians, "Be angry but do not sin. Do not let the sun go down on your anger, and give no opportunity to the devil" (Eph. 4:26). I understand this to mean that unexpressed and denied anger are likely to turn into the wrath that can do the devil's work, whereas anger functioning as a sign of truth, revealing fear and hurt between us, can lead to reconciliation, which is God's work in the world (see 2 Cor. 5:16; Eph. 1:10).

Does this understanding of anger accord with the story of Jesus in the Gospels, so that in him we can again see the "pioneer and perfecter" of this hardest of all virtues? I think so. We are familiar with Jesus' most obvious expression of anger: his driving the money changers out of the Temple (Mark 11:15-17). The text does not actually *say* that Jesus was angry, but it is difficult to imagine the deed being carried out with *apatheia*. John, in fact, tells us that Jesus used a whip and shouted at the bankers (John 2:15-17). We notice that Jesus' anger in this instance was immediate and properly directed. He is angry at *them*, for what they are doing to the honor of his Father's house. His anger is appropriately expressed, for he removes the offense without doing violence to them as persons. Notice that he does not (as does the Qumran community) erect his anger into a hostile project against the Temple as such or its unworthy priesthood.

The anger of Jesus can be sensed as well in his exorcisms. He *rebukes* the unclean spirits, has no patience with them, will not let them speak, drives them out (see Mark 1:25; 5:8). His anger in this case is directed at the forces that bind other humans and is appropriately expressed by releasing captive persons from their torment. Jesus' anger is explicitly expressed in the story of his healing on the Sabbath a man who had a withered hand. Jesus asks his opponents, who are watching him, whether it is lawful to do good on the Sabbath. They keep silent, a classic passive-aggressive response. Mark 3:5 notes, "He looked around at them with anger, grieved at their hardness of heart."

When analyzing the obedience of faith, I traced the narrative in Mark's Gospel concerning Jesus' attempt to follow one project of preaching while everyone wanted from him a ministry of healing (Mark 1:29-37). We saw that when Peter tells Jesus, "Everyone is seeking you," Jesus responds promptly with a reassertion of his project as he then understands it. He refuses to stay in that village to heal people: "Let us go on to the next towns, that I may preach there also; for that is why I came out (1:38). Jesus carries out that project; he preaches in all the synagogues of Galilee (1:39). But Mark places as the very next incident in the story the request of the leper for healing, "If you will, you can make me clean" (1:40). Jesus no sooner forms his project and tries to carry it out than he is interrupted and challenged by this sick person who is truly "other," removed by his stigma from society.

Most translations of the New Testament have as Jesus' response something close to the Revised Standard Version: "Moved with pity, he stretched out his hand and touched him, and said to him, 'I will; be clean' " (Mark 1:41). Some ancient Greek manuscripts have quite a different reading in this place, such a hard reading, in fact, that I tend to favor its authenticity. They have not *splanknistheis*— "moved with pity"—but *orgistheis*, "moved with *anger*." This has always seemed to me to be exactly right. I recognize in this version the natural reaction to the demand of another that we step out of our project: we resist it; we experience anger. Thus, confronted again with the demand to heal, Jesus is angry. But he responds to the call, reaches out, and heals. He enters into the dark place that is God's project for his messiahship, which he cannot control. The leper ends up back in society; Jesus ends up in the desert, unable to preach, and besieged even more by those seeking him there (1:45). In this passage we learn how Jesus, though Son, "learned obedience through what he suffered," and that part of what he suffered was the emotion of anger.

Sexuality and Agapē

Although we sometimes find it difficult to laugh, most of us can agree that there is good evidence for the Creator's rich humor in that humanity is distributed between two genders. Genesis tells us clearly that it was *as* male and female that God created humans in the divine image and blessed them (Gen. 1:27-28). Most men and women have had a hard time perceiving that image clearly, and have tended to regard their sexual differentiation as at best a mixed blessing. The Genesis myth vividly shows how human sin was expressed by hostility between the sexes. Disobedience to God leads to the breaking of trust and fidelity between humans: "The woman . . . gave me fruit of the tree, and I ate" (3:12). The result is not only a sense of shame at nakedness (3:10) and the pain of childbirth (3:16) to confuse the human experience of sexuality, but even more a complex combination of attraction and revulsion between women and men that is never entirely unambiguous: "Your desire shall be for your husband, and he shall rule over you" (3:16).

Nowhere is the complexity of doing the truth in love more evident than in the relations between women and men. For the majority of persons—leaving aside the even more difficult issue of homosexuality—sexual differentiation means physical attraction. It is by no means clear, however, what (if anything) connects the powerful impetus toward unity generated by *eros* to the willing the good of the other, which is *agapē*. Are they even compatible? Neither is it clear that women and men can have *philia*, the love of friendship, between them. Are they capable of sharing interests in the way demanded by true friendship, or are their interests always opposed? Do men and women represent, in effect, two forms of humanity that have so little in common that they are fated to a sometimes humorous, but more often tragic, war between the sexes? Is there any clarity available in this confusion between "desire" and "rule" (Gen. 3:16)?

As if these basic problems were not enough, Christianity has made the issue of sexuality even more difficult. Jesus, we declare, revealed the meaning of *agapē* (1 John 4:10). But the New Testament gives no reason to think that Jesus was sexually active. He died a violent death while still youthful. Then he was experienced as living more powerfully in the Spirit among believers. All of this made the Messiah at best an ambiguous sexual exemplar.

The Gnostic Model. Not surprisingly, the models of Christian spirituality have suggested ways of simplifying the relation of *agapē* to sexuality. We can begin to locate a healthier way of thinking about mature Christian sexuality by considering in turn their respective oversimplifications. The gnostic model of spirituality regards sexuality problematic most of all because of the element of desire. The strong version of this spirituality regarded the body itself as evil, the product of a malicious demiurge opposed to the spiritual God. If women and men united sexually, they would be celebrating by their physicality the "work of the creator" and thereby be cooperating with the evil god. That would be bad enough, but if they also had children, they would perpetuate and extend that evil, generating even more materiality to imprison souls. In this version, only two sexual options were available to Christians. The first was obvious: to avoid sexual activity altogether, so that celibacy and Christianity were synonymous. The second was more subtle: to mock the creator god by manipulating sexuality for pleasure but not for procreation.

The weaker version of the gnostic model remained standard for much of Christian spirituality. This version located the problem not in the intrinsic evil of the body but in its power to control the mind. Sexual desire and activity is confusing. Attraction, arousal, passion: these are all antithetic to the classic ideal of *apatheia*. In this understanding, *eros* and *agapē* are virtually incompatible. Christian love is based on free choice; but *eros* is all disruptive blind drive. Patristic writers made desire or concupiscence the very seat of sin. The remnants of that conviction are evident in the popular equation of sin with sex.

Sexual arousal and activity are therefore avoided for the safety of the soul. If sexual activity means the loss of rational control, then it is better eschewed altogether. The "state of perfection" is found in a celibate commitment. The sexual ideal is virginity. The goal of spirituality is the killing of the animal within, or at the very least its domestication. The saint is not only sexually inactive; the saint has no sexual desire at all. This model can appeal in the most obvious way to the example of Jesus, of whose sexuality the Gospels give not a clue.

As in the case of anger, however, the systematic denial or repression of a natural bodily function has disastrous results. The multiple ways in which the sexual drive can camouflage and transform itself have been exhaustively catalogued by psychoanalysis. If anything, the danger of denial and repression in this area has become almost too common a part of conventional wisdom. Many younger Christians take it for granted that sexual abstinence is itself unhealthy. Bolder libertines even look at sublimation with suspicion. Sexual expression and satisfaction is peddled as a cure-all for physical and emotional dysfunction. The pansexualism of contemporary culture is obviously sub-Christian. What little credibility it possesses, however, derives from the clear damage done by the gnostic model of spirituality.

The Liberation Model. The liberation model also has problems with sexual differentiation but for different reasons. The problem now is defined not in terms of desire but in terms of power. It focuses on the way gender distinctions have been translated into social roles and statuses that are at best unequal and at worst oppressive and destructive. The problem is summarized again by Gen. 3:16: "he shall rule over you." Throughout history, men have dominated and frequently oppressed women. The pattern, it is claimed, has not been changed by Christianity and may in fact have been made worse. The villain in this case is Paul, who is regarded at least as sexist and quite probably as misogynist. The so-called "tables of household ethics" (Col. 3:18—4:1; Eph. 5:21—6:9), which command wives to "be submissive to your husbands," are taken as emblematic of the subjection of women within the church.

The Teaching of Paul

Conservative and liberationist social programs once more agree on their reading of the texts, but with quite different valuations. Fundamentalist Christians justify the subordination of women in church and home by appeal to these texts of Paul. They show little embarrassment at passages seeming to suggest either inferiority of nature or of character in women (1 Cor. 11:3, 8; 1 Tim. 2:14). These same texts are the ones which repel Christians who take the feminist agenda as a basic moral and social commitment.

Some feminists maintain a connection to Christianity by appealing to other passages in Paul such as his statement that in Christ "there is neither male nor female" (Gal. 3:28) or to the example of Jesus as a woman-defined man. For others, the sexism of the New Testament and Christian tradition are too difficult to negotiate. They call for a "Womanchurch" that maintains the claim to be authentically Christian but which bases itself on a feminist reading of the tradition. Others, finally, abandon Christianity altogether as a lost cause.

I want to argue that Paul is not the villain in this piece, but rather a misreading of Paul within *both* the gnostic and liberation models that distorts this aspect of Christian spirituality. I will try to provide a reading of Paul that responds to their oversimplifications of human sexual identity. Paul refuses to reduce sexuality either to *desire* or to *power*. He considers sexuality as a fundamental aspect of our human self-disposition in freedom, therefore as an aspect of the obedience of faith and the doing of truth in love.

The New Creation.   Paul discusses the relationship between sexual behavior and the kingdom most extensively in 1 Corinthians 7. We have already noted the premise for his entire discussion of "life in the world" (7:28-35): the passing away of the frame of this world demands an eschatological detachment. Christians are neither to flee the world or construct an alternative world, but are to engage the normal world of human experience. They are to do this from the distinctive perspective given by faith: the world is not itself ultimate or a closed system. It is created at every moment by the living God and is answerable to God. It is a world, furthermore, that has entered into a "new age" or "new creation" (2 Cor. 5:16) in virtue of the resurrection of Jesus.

This premise governs Paul's discussion of sexuality. His community had written him a letter asking for his advice (1 Cor. 7:1). The first issue they raised concerned sexual behavior in the church, posed by one of their easy slogans, "It is well for a man not to touch a woman." Although Paul takes that statement as his starting point, he does not agree with it. The rest of his discussion serves to narrow the applicability of that radical statement. Paul does not offer support for a gnostic denigration of the body or of sexuality. His preference for celibacy (for those who have the gift) is entirely connected to serving the community's work (the "affairs of the Lord," 7:32), especially in the conditions of the end-time, since being married means care for those whom one loves (7:32-34). But, says Paul, if a celibate is preoccupied by sexual desires anyway (7:2, 9), it is better to marry.

Marriage, in fact, is the state that Paul regards as usual. The resurrection life in the Spirit does not utterly replace the order of nature. Because of the crucified and raised Messiah, the blessings of God can no longer be understood simply in temporal terms; Christians cannot regard married love and long life and many off-spring as absolute goods. On the other hand, Christians do not yet share fully in the resurrection of the dead (1 Corinthians 15), a state, Jesus said, when humans "neither marry nor are given in marriage, . . . because they are equal to angels and are sons of God, being sons of the resurrection" (Luke 20:35-36). The sexual project of marriage is regarded by Paul as appropriate and good. In fact, he reaffirms the commandment of Jesus forbidding divorce (7:10-11), allowing the possibility of separation only for reasons of spiritual incompatibility (7:15).

Paul does not think of marriage as a "property arrangement," but as a powerful covenantal relationship, in which sexual intimacy and spiritual communion are explicitly connected. He obviously approves of the intimacy of *eros* and does not see it as incompatible with *agapē*. Wife and husband are not to be "brother and sister" to each other, although they are so in the community and before the Lord (7:15). Their active sexual relationship should not be interrupted except for purposes of prayer, and then only temporarily (7:5). The physical union between female and male powerfully influences both. The wife can sanctify the husband. Parents can also sanctify their children by their married love (7:14).

The possibility of spiritual transformation through a sexual relationship is based in the psychosomatic character of human freedom. Paul condemns Christians who frequent prostitutes (1 Cor. 6:15), not because sex is ugly but because sex is distorted when it eliminates the dimension of personal engagement in knowledge and love. The physical embrace of humans is meant to symbolize spiritual unity as well. Prostitution mocks this symbolism. The Corinthians defend their practice by quoting another of their slogans, "Food is meant for the stomach, the stomach for food" (6:13). They think that sex is like eating, is a physical phenomenon only, a closed system. Paul rejects their premise. Sexual love is meant to involve the uniting of knowledge and love; promiscuity is wrong because it omits this essential spiritual dimension (1 Cor. 6:16).

Paul's discussion in 1 Corinthians 7 asserts sexuality as a positive aspect of God's creation. Like the use of power and possessions, Christians are to use their sexual capacities with eschatological freedom. Paul's discussion also asserts the equality between male and female before God. Notice the subtle dynamics of Paul's discussion. He addresses himself consistently to *both* female and male readers, giving them equal attention when considering specific cases. Men are not spoken to as though they were the ones who made decisions; women are given the same options as men. Only two instances address the male exclusively. We have already seen that the opening declaration, "it is well for a man not to touch a woman" (7:1), is not Paul's own opinion. The other statement takes up the case of a man marrying his betrothed (7:36-38). Otherwise, throughout this whole discussion, Paul matches every statement concerning men with another pertaining to women; they have absolutely equal rights and obligations in the relationship (see 7:4-5, 10-11, 12-13, 14, 15-16, 27-28, 33-34). The entire discussion concludes with a statement concerning the essential freedom of the widow: her dignity does not depend on her being attached to a man (7:39-40).

Equality and Social Status.   Paul's perception of sexual equality is not simply rhetorical. It is based on principle. Paul makes several distinctions of fundamental importance for understanding relations between female and male. He first distinguishes the call to Christian identity, which is the same for all, and each person's "special gift from God" (1 Cor. 7:7) which are diverse and intended not for self-assertion over against others, but for the building up of the community (see especially 12:4-11). This distinction establishes an absolute equality within the Christian community concerning membership and obligation. It defines differences between members not in terms of worth but in terms of service. Otherness in the gifts is important because we are saved by the grace of otherness, the diversity of gifts together build the body of the Messiah (12:12-13). Neither the celibate nor the married can claim superiority. Both married and celibate are called to serve the community by their individual ways of living out their sexual identity.

Paul's second distinction is between Christian identity and social status. The "call of God" (7:17) is absolute and unconditional; every Christian is of equal status before God, and must equally "keep the commandments of God" (7:19). The call and mandate are unaffected by race, social position, or gender. Paul uses the examples of "neither circumcised nor uncircumcised" (neither Jew nor Greek) and of "neither slave nor free" (7:18-23). In context, however, his intended application to the relationship between male and female is unmistakeable. No specific social condition can keep one from the call of God, and none inhibits "keeping the commandments." Social differences remain. For Paul, it appears, the fact of such differences are critical to the church. Differences are the presupposition to unity. But social differences (including the basic categories of gender, race, and status) are *relativized*. They are not to distinguish the worth *or* the function of members within the body. The worth comes from God's call. The function comes from the gift of God's Spirit "who apportions to each one individually as he wills," (12:11), and "to each is given the manifestation of the Spirit for the common good" (12:7).

Paul's distinctions are especially pertinent because they tend to be denied in the liberation model. If human worth and social status (the possession of certain rights) are equated, then a woman holding a socially subordinate position truly does have her dignity damaged. She will not be "fully human" until the power ratio with men is equal. Paul counters that position when he addresses the issue of slavery: "The one who was called in the Lord as a slave is a freedman of the Lord. Likewise he who was free when called is a slave of Christ" (7:22). Being "in Christ" or "in the Lord" means for Paul being in a "new creation" (2 Cor. 5:17), and both phrases figure in other texts in which Paul discusses relations between the genders.

One of his most troublesome passages is 1 Cor. 11:1-16. Paul demands that when they pray or prophesy in the assembly, women should wear veils. He is obviously emotionally exercised by the topic; he brings forward one argument after another: The nature of things (11:3;14); the sequence of creation (11:7); social propriety (11:5; 13). But it quickly becomes clear that Paul has no reason that even he finds compelling, since he ends by invoking the custom of the churches (11:16). Paul himself can find no *principled* objection to women prophesying or praying without veils, but only *customary usage*. But if we are in the realm of custom, then we are obviously in the realm of (at least possible) change.

The passage illustrates the tension, endemic to Christianity, between an egalitarian ideal and the demands of social structure for order and authority. Paul in this case struggles to assert the social convention for the sake of consistency and order. His own convictions concerning the messianic community prevent him making a good case. In 1 Cor. 11:8 he tries to support his position: "Man was not made from woman, but woman from man. Neither was man created for woman, but woman for man." This is a straightforward reading of the Genesis account: Eve was taken from Adam's side to be his helpmate. So Paul concludes "that is why a woman ought to wear a veil." But *immediately*, he remembers that they no longer live simply in the realm of nature but in a new creation. Paul is therefore compelled to add: "Nevertheless, in the Lord, woman is not independent of man nor man of woman; for as woman was made from man, so man is now born of woman. And all things are from God" (1 Cor. 11:11-12). With this, Paul has effectively blocked any appeal to principle, and must fall back on custom.

The same tension characterizes all Paul's statements concerning the sexes. When Paul is addressing the central issues of identity in the community, his defense of radical equality is direct and emphatic. Thus, in the Galatian controversy, Paul responds to the attempts of Judaizing Christians to demand circumcision as a higher stage of initiation into the "mysteries of Moses," by asserting the relativization of all such distinctions in the community. "There is neither Jew nor Greek, there is neither slave nor free, there is neither male nor female; for you are all one in Christ Jesus" (Gal. 3:28). The full implications of including "male and female" in the statement are too seldom noted. If circumcision had been established as a further and better stage of initiation, it would obviously be available only to males. By fighting the circumcisers, Paul fought the first (if unconscious) feminist battle within Christianity.

Paul's understanding of the difference that the messianic pattern makes for men and women informs his statement of household ethics less directly. In these traditional moral instructions for the standard kinship system in the Hellenistic world, Paul not only emphasizes the reciprocity of obligations between the power relationships of husband/wife, parent/child, master/free, but also relativizes the demand for submission from the lower members of each pair (wives, children, slaves) by using the phrase "in the Lord" (Col. 3:18, 20, 22; Eph. 6:1). As elsewhere, this means that any submission to a social structure must be subordinate to the higher claim of faith's obedience to God. The absolute claim of the social order is relativized by the demand of the gospel. Only in Eph. 5:21 does Paul's language tend to strengthen the force of the social obligations, telling wives to give obedience to their husbands "as to the Lord." But even in that passage, the higher mandate of the relationship to

God is clearly stated (see especially 6:5-9), and in any case, Paul was trying to make another point in Eph. 5:21-32.

Learning from Paul

The problem of the power relationship between the genders was obviously not solved by Paul. But at least he saw the problem and dealt with it creatively. As a man coming from the systematically patriarchal tradition of Pharisaism, it is in fact remarkable that the Spirit could bring him so far. What is perhaps more surprising is that we have made so little progress since Paul, so that he still has something to teach us. Paul presents a genuine challenge to contemporary Christians who wish at the same time to be true to the Christian tradition (and texts) and to their perceptions (shaped by hard experience) that the systematic oppression of women by men, either through the overt practice of violence or through the covert means of economic and political manipulation, must stop. The challenge is that they take with the same seriousness Paul did both poles of the inevitable tension between relational equality and the demands of social structure. Like Paul, we live in kinship groups that require definition, boundaries, and decision-making procedures (authority). Like Paul, we need to apply to our kinship systems the best philosophical teaching available to us, just as he applied the moral teaching of stoicism to the kinship system of the Hellenistic household. But also like Paul, we must refuse to absolutize either our social arrangement or our ideology. We must, like him, allow the more fundamental claim of the Gospel to loosen our claim to have the final version of the kingdom, and add to our arrangements as well the implicit critique of life in the Lord.

Paul has not solved the problem of human sexuality, but he has taught us to think of sexuality less as a problem than as an aspect of the mystery of our embodied freedom. By insisting both on the reality and goodness of sexual activity because of creation *and* on the relativization of any sexual project because of the resurrection-life in the Lord, Paul has recognized a tension that will not be resolved theoretically but only by real women and men who shape communities of knowledge and love and who symbolize them in diverse ways by the disposition of their bodies. By insisting both on the fundamental equality of female and male in the Lord *and* on the inevitable power disparities inherent in social structures, Paul also acknowledges a tension that can never be utterly escaped but must be renegotiated in every generation by men and women alike. In principle, however, this negotiation must take place "by agreement" (1 Cor. 7:5) between partners of equal status in the Lord, whose identity and worth as brother and sister transcend the social roles of husband and wife.

This discussion of sexuality might seem to be far from the topic of "doing the truth in love." In fact, however, the complex intertanglings of desire and power that are unavoidably part of our sexual existence are part of the truth of our life together, and must therefore be acknowledged before we can claim to have *agapē* toward each other as female and male. Because of the complexities of desire and power, both women and men must place their sexual projects within obedient faith. They can form their own projects, but must allow them to be relativized by the projects of the other. They must take the other's interests into account as well as their own (Phil. 2:4).

Because of their historical and cultural conditionings, men and women tend to have the opposite temptations in this respect. Men tend toward willfulness, making their own projects absolute, overriding those of women, often not even recognizing that women have legitimate projects of their own that are not defined by their relationship to the male. Women, in contrast, tend toward willlessness, for the sake of acceptance and love fitting themselves to the projects of men and refusing to form projects of their own. They are thereby not more faithful but simply more alienated. Paul would insist, I think, that *both* men and women need to form projects and at the same time be attentive to those of the other.

Placing the relationship between the sexes in the context of obedient faith enables us to better appreciate two positive aspects of the otherness of the sexes. The first is simply that if we are graced by otherness, as I have argued in this book, then in the most obvious way men and women are gifts to each other. It is in their differentness, their having diverse perceptions, sensibilities, and projects, that they challenge each other and offer each other the opportunity to grow. By shaping her own identity and project, by refusing to simply submit herself to the man's project, the woman not only looks to her own interests but *also* serves the interest of the man; for she provides him the chance to grow beyond his own narrow world into a larger understanding of what it means to be human. The man does the same thing for the woman. What is required of both, of course, is attentive listening and the willingness to have the private projects enlarged by such hearing of the other. The tragedy of "Men Only Clubs" and of "Womanchurch" alike is that they both diminish the humanity of their members by closing off the possibility of growth.

But when men and women do the truth in love by placing their respective desires and projects of power within the context of obedient faith, discerning together the call of God in the world, the reconciliation between the sexes can mean the restoration of the image of God in humanity. This is surely what Paul means in Eph. 5:32, when he says of the love between man and woman, "This mystery is a profound one," and refers it directly to "Christ and the church."

Paul's entire argument in Ephesians involves God's plan to unify all things in Christ (Eph. 1:10). The sign of human estrangement from God is hostility between people (2:3). Paul points to the hostility between Jew and Gentile as the historical paradigm of sinful alienation (2:11-12). The death and resurrection of Jesus was meant to heal that division, creating a new humanity on the basis of his faithful obedience and sacrificial love (2:14-16). The church, Paul says, is the sacrament of that reconciliation, its effective sign. It is the place where God's will for the world is revealed (3:8-11). This means that the church must be a place of reconciliation, a place where Jew and Gentile meet as equals and as part of the "one body in the Spirit" (2:16-18). Paul could not, in other words, conceive a church that was *in principle* only Jewish or only Gentile, only black or only white, only heterosexual or only homosexual, only rich or only poor, only male or only female. There must be differences for there to be unity (4:4-13). And only if the church is a community which realizes such reconciliation can it symbolize God's will for the world and offer the world a genuine alternative to its destructive hostility based on differences.

Paul obviously regards the split between male and female as real and as grievous as that between Jew and Greek and slave and free. He reverts time and again to the negative side of the Genesis story (1 Cor. 11:8-9; 2 Cor. 11:3; 1 Tim. 2:13-14). But the Genesis story is also capable of another reading, says Paul, in light of the New Adam who is Christ (Eph. 5:31). The self-emptying love between man and woman can symbolize the other reconciliations. If the church by reconciling Jew and Greek is called to be a sacrament to the world of the possibility of peace between nations, then the love of man and woman can be a sacrament to the church itself (Eph. 5:32), by effecting an even more fundamental sort of peace, the restoration of the image of God in humans: "In the image of God he created him; male and female he created them" (Gen. 1:27).

9

Christian Realism:
Evil and Suffering

C hristian maturity demands seeing the world as it truly is. There is nothing particularly holy about refusing to see the dark side of reality or denying the evil and suffering in the world. Nothing in fact can so quickly discredit faith as its parody, the cheery chirp that "God's in his heaven and all's well with the world," or the slick slogan slapped in the face of appalling disaster, "God works everything to the good for those who love him." Mature faith demands acknowledging not only that God creates the world at every moment, but also that *in our experience of it*, the world is not altogether as it should be.

It is important to state that *faith* itself incorporates this perception, for some critics make a "realistic" perception of the world (one that sees all its evil and suffering) the very antithesis of faith. In its most primitive form, this either/or is found in adults who gave up faith in their childhood, because they had prayed really hard for something, did not get it, and concluded that belief in God was on a par with belief in Santa Claus; further disillusionment could only be avoided by total skepticism. In another version, a youth tests God's powers (of observation and recrimination) by going to an empty field, shaking a fist at the sky and cursing God. Since nothing happens, he concludes that God cannot see or cannot act, and in either case, is worth no further consideration.

At a more reflective level, the presence of evil and suffering in the world has long been a classic moral argument against faith in a loving God, and remains the strongest motivation for what can be called principled atheism. The argument in this case is put in terms of logical opposition. Either God is powerless or God is not loving. If God were loving and all powerful, God would not allow evil and suffering. Alternatively, if God were all powerful and yet allowed evil and suffering, God could not be loving. If God does exist, therefore, it is either as morally bankrupt or as a powerless onlooker; in either case God is not much use in our grim contest for survival.

People who maintain faith in the face of evil and suffering adopt various strategies, dependent in large measure on their perception of God's relationship with the world. Some deal with their loss of innocence by withdrawing from active involvement with the world in order to maintain their own integrity and that of the interior God. In an isolationist spirituality, they seek a garden within. Others withdraw into communities of other good people, letting the suffering and evil out in the world go its own way. In their utopian communes, they seek a garden apart. Such are the classic responses of a gnostic spirituality; it flees the world.

The response of a liberation spirituality, in contrast, is to battle the evil social systems that entrap humans, reforming the world into what it ought to be, literally recreating it in the image of an ideal humanity. In the strong, Marxist/Leninist version of this spirituality of revolution, the essential premise is that belief in God is, in and of itself, alienating. Faith blinds people to the true causes of their suffering. To truly engage and recreate the world, therefore, one must begin by repudiating faith in God. The lightly baptized Christian version of this spirituality uses a process version of God. Belief in a loving God is saved by identifying God with the human activity of social reform. Quite literally in this view, God is what we make of the world.

The gnostic and liberation responses to evil and suffering work only by eliminating one or the other side of the tension. Either God goes, or the world does. Behind this collapse lies the same inability to join God's power or love to the evil and suffering we experience in the world. If we are to make progress in our thinking, therefore, and find a way for mature faith to maintain both God and world, we must begin by recognizing the difficulty of identifying precisely what we mean by evil and suffering. If ever definitions were essential, it is here. Yet in this discussion above all, precision in language seems most to be lacking. My analysis here begins with a recognition of the easy and misleading equations all of us tend to use for rhetorical purposes, above all the equation of evil and suffering.

The Denial of Evil

Three tendencies of our ordinary language deserve particular attention. The first is the way we exercise rhetorical overkill and as a result destroy delicate and important distinctions between *levels* and *kinds* of human misfortune (to use a neutral term). The most obvious example is the way we appropriate the terms used to describe one event which is inarguably evil in order to heighten horror at some other event: the local sheriff is the Gestapo; school detention is Dachau; someone who tells a racist joke is a Hitler; the death of some soldiers is a Holocaust. Our language and perceptions alike are thereby trivialized. Many of us also use the language of suffering in manipulative ways, assuming that suffering is always and everywhere evil. We speak more or less indiscriminately of the suffering parents, the suffering children, the suffering peasants, the suffering whales, and suffering laboratory animals in order to evoke an instant *moral* response to *evil*. Because we are unrestrained in language, we erase critical distinctions. If psoriasis is a heartbreak, what is the loss of a loved one? If losing a football game is a tragedy, what can we call the death of a child, or famine or pestilence? If saving petroleum is the moral equivalent of war, how does this affect our perception of the war on poverty or the war on drugs?

Another tendency in our discussions is the removal of evil from the realm of human freedom. On one side, we demonize evil—either in the traditional sense of the evil one operating in the world, or in the liberation sense of demonic social structures. Human responsibility for specific evil actions is eliminated. The notion of collective responsibility corrodes rather than strengthens the sense of personal responsibility. On the other side, we psychologize evil. We make evil a species of sickness, and therefore, a kind of suffering. If Hitler can be shown to be sick then he was not responsible for his deeds. But if he was not responsible, how could he be evil? Only by being a demon. And if even that does not suit, we can always invoke the mysterious sickness of the German nation.

By eliminating evil as a category of human freedom we have also in one bold stroke removed sin from our moral lexicon (for there cannot be personal sin without freedom). With equal panache, we have shifted guilt from the realm of an objective statement concerning human responsibility to the psychological area of unhealthy feelings. A major step in getting healthy, we assure each other, is the elimination of neurotic guilt feelings. One of the very few remaining social offenses is to make someone feel guilty, or force them on a guilt trip.

Within this peculiar looking-glass world more and more of us inhabit, any evil we do is accountable by the fact that we ourselves are victims (of genes, environment, nurture, early abuse, sexist/racist/imperialist culture, and so forth). If we are victims, it is somehow assumed, we are free from moral responsibility. We are, rather, among those who suffer. Both those murdered in cold blood and their slayers are sufferers. But the slain suffered only for a moment; their pitiful slayers continue to suffer and require our therapeutic rather than our punitive attention. Among the nasty illogicalities in this train of equations is this one: moral suffering depends on a conscience, a sense of right and wrong and of personal responsibility. Without that, it is perfectly possible to be at one and the same time thoroughly evil and thoroughly happy.

In our usual way of talking about suffering and evil we also oversimplify the relationship of God to the world. We speak of God as though God were not only the primary but the sole cause at work in the world. We also pretend to know the meaning of terms such as justice when applied to God. The first oversimplification is found among the faith's apologists as well as its detractors. A special category of events called acts of God is used to prove beneficent power or powerless malice. For the apologist, a miracle can come only from God directly, apart from human causality. Healings are therefore used to prove God's direct intervention and loving power. Negative events such as earthquakes and epidemics offer themselves to the same interpretation. The apologist might call them punishment for sin (as recently in the case of the AIDS epidemic), but with only limited success. It might work for Sodom and Gomorrah, but what about earthquakes in Armenia? So long as deviant sex or drug addiction are perceived as the sole causes of AIDS, we might want to invoke the theme of punishment for sin. But what about the heterosexual mothers and newborn infants who are indiscriminately infected with the same fatal virus? From the opposite side, the detractor of faith seizes on the suffering of the innocent in such events as famines, wars, persecutions, epidemics, and floods to prove with equal logic that God is either powerless to prevent evil (*that* equation again) or worse, *allows* or *causes* evil.

This approach has a simplistic understanding of causality. Is God's effect in the world any less real when it is carried out through secondary causes, after all? Is the hammering of the nail any less due to me if I use a hammer rather than my fist? The approach also is acontextual. How are we to evaluate this special event attributed to God's direct action apart from all the other events in which God is also at work? This leads me to the second kind of oversimplification. We tend to use language univocally, forgetting that our language about God is always at best analogical and demands as a first step a negation of our ordinary language. Precisely because we do not know the whole are we prevented from a final judgment on the justice or injustice, the goodness or evil of *God's* causality in a specific event. Yet God is precisely and by definition related to the whole of creation.

It may be good for us to remember that, despite the enormous growth in our knowledge of the natural world, we still are far from maker's knowledge. In our perception of the earth's whole ecosystem, we are still largely in the realm of guesswork concerning effects (as in the case of the ozone layer and the greenhouse effect), as well as causes. We cannot even accurately predict all the consequences of our interventions in the order of nature. What we struggle to know, furthermore, we grasp only for this moment and this small planet. And in our learning, we actually discover what was planned by an antecedent and infinitely greater intelligence. Even as we approach knowing the whole at the physical/biological level, we must acknowledge that much of our understanding comes from the ways in which we have distorted or destroyed (by our freedom, by our making in technology) a system more perfect than we can replace. It is a bit pretentious for we who consistently fail to understand justice in human affairs to rush to judgment concerning God's way in the world.

This is not a call to a blind fideism that shuts its eyes to the world. Just the opposite; it is required of mature faith to abandon naivete and to think with great seriousness about suffering and evil. But such thinking must take place at the level of reflection rather than that of problem solving, for we have to do with the mystery of human existence, a mystery from which we cannot detach ourselves as disinterested observers. To think about suffering and evil means to confront not only our personal and communal suffering, but also the evil that we ourselves do. We cannot simply identify ourselves as sufferers and victims and enjoy the pleasures of innocence. We are all involved in the same drama of idolatry and grace, sin and faith, in which our human freedom is articulated and for which we are responsible. The proper way to begin thinking, then, may be to admit that we are incapable of perfect clarity and unambiguous conclusions, precisely because we are creatures in process who have not yet concluded our participation in the drama. But having acknowledged that, we cannot abandon reason. Indeed, the best way to proceed is by performing the act our minds do best: making distinctions. The most important distinction of all must structure the entire discussion. If we are thinking through the *Christian* understanding of life, then it is essential that we *not* simply identify suffering and evil.

Thinking about Evil

Our confusion concerning evil is reflected in the very word. I pick up my old battered *Webster's New Collegiate Dictionary* and look at the adjective, "evil," and find it defined as "not good morally; wicked" and "arising from actual or imputed bad character or conduct." Yet as a noun, evil is defined as "something that brings sorrow, distress, or calamity"; and "the fact of suffering and misfortune"; and, "a cosmic evil force." In other words, it is a term that shifts in usage between the very poles that I am trying to keep separate.

As a cosmic evil force evil is sometimes used to name the personified agent of moral wickedness (Satan). In some forms of Christianity, talk about Satan is a dominant feature. It is part of the demonizing of evil that I earlier deplored. Insofar as it deflects moral responsibility away from humans themselves ("The devil made me do it") or prevents them from dealing with the moral ambiguities of their own behavior, such language is self-alienating. Another aspect of such language is the way it demarcates parts of the world as belonging to the evil one. Strongly sectarian Christianity tends to agree with John: "We know that we are of God, and the whole world is in the power of the evil one" (1 John 5:19). It uses this sentiment to justify the rejection of any good offered by secular society and the construction of alternative Christian social forms. By so doing, however, it distorts the fundamental Christian perception of God as the Creator and ruler of all the world, no part of which is simply ruled by Satan.

The cosmic evil force can also refer to some actual part of the world. In the strong gnostic version of Christianity, both the material universe and the god who created it were by definition evil, because they imprisoned souls in bodies and kept them alienated from their true identity in the Light. Weaker versions of the gnostic model refrained from actually designating the body as evil, but they certainly treated it as though it were the source and cause of evil. Contemporary secular versions of Gnosticism likewise identify certain substances, such as carcinogenics, as evil in themselves, to be avoided in however minute quantities.

It is far more common today to find evil used to refer to the fact of suffering or misfortune. The pedigree of this identification is impressive; it forms the starting point for the Buddhist Four Noble Truths which provide a liberation from the suffering that derives from imprisonment in the body with its senses, its desires, and false ego-identity. In the common form of this equation, any suffering is simply regarded as evil, without a great deal of distinction. A wide variety of human experiences can count: the disappointment of desire or failure of expectations; physical injury or mutilation or sickness or death; mental anguish or uncertainty; emotional trauma. The common denominator for suffering is *pain*, whether physical, mental, or emotional. Even the pain of animals, sometimes even the pain of plants, is included within the evil that is suffering.

This equation is fraught with problems, not the least of which is that it mixes an absolute category with a relative one. However we define it, evil must stand as an absolute term. Evil is not something to which we can morally assent, or which we can choose. Suffering, in contrast, is a polyvalent term. Not only are there relative degrees of suffering, and different kinds of suffering, but suffering can serve, as we shall see, positive functions. Some suffering is inevitable as part of the process of nature; all material things tend toward corruption, and for sentient beings that process is accompanied by pain. But suffering is also an accompaniment to positive growth, as an organism stretches to a new level of being or awareness. Humans can in fact choose a relative suffering for the sake of what they perceive to be a greater good: greater pleasure, or usefulness, or beauty, or virtue. But they must not so directly and deliberately choose evil that good may come. The valuation of suffering, therefore, must depend on the context in which it occurs. But if suffering *can* be a good, then it should not simply be equated with evil.

I am not trying to minimize the importance of the suffering that is *not* freely chosen, or is inflicted, or is experienced as a destructive force. Suffering can also *be* an evil, as I hope to show. But some suffering does not possess that moral or religious valuation as such. We need, therefore, to maintain some rigor in our language concerning such experiences. We can call some human experiences (and the experiences of other species) unfortunate or sad, or tragic, or— to use the most appropriate sort of language—awful (generating awe) and terrible (creating terror). This language describes the emotional and mental impact made on us by the sight or the experience of suffering. We should, however, be more careful about invoking the category of evil.

More than linguistic purity is at stake. When we grow careless in our understanding of evil and suffering, we lose as well some of the depth of our perception of life. Surely it is a common theme today that suffering is wrong. We speak of many young and not-so-young people in the contemporary world as having been raised with a sense of entitlement. One of the premises of that outlook is that life should not contain suffering, that the world ought to be gracious and accepting, that human experience should be without risk and free from pain. Not only does such an outlook (enabled and encouraged by a consumer technology) create persons of peculiarly soft sensibilities, acutely aware of their own rights (misusing this term as well) and how they are slighted by vaguely amorphous others who are keeping them from reaching their full potential (the only remaining sin), and persons who are increasingly incapable of expending the energy (and feeling the pain) required for real growth and excellence; it makes Christianity appear bizarre and incomprehensible. How could suffering for others be a sign of mature love, if suffering is always an evil?

Evil and Sin.   The proper location for our language about evil is in connection with human freedom, specifically in that disposition of freedom called sin. In my earlier discussion, I distinguished sin from idolatry (although both were distortions of creation) by emphasizing the *choice* character of sin. Sin is idolatry chosen in face of a real option. Sin is precisely the expression of evil because it lies in the face of truth, chooses blindness rather than sight, seeks to do harm rather than good. Sin elevates the pattern of self-aggrandizement and hostility into an absolute and aggressive force in the world.

People do sin. We must begin with that simple declaration. We cannot explain sin or reduce it to something else, like sickness or confusion. Augustine called sin the "mystery of iniquity," precisely because it is hard to understand how or why persons would reject the gift of knowledge and love from another and choose rather to distort and destroy. But they do—we do—and the first step toward genuine Christian realism is to acknowledge sin, not simply as an abstract possibility but as the concrete context for much of our lives in the world. People act selfishly and destructively. They seek their own pleasure at the expense of others' survival. They add to their wealth to the dispossession of others. They lie and cheat and steal. They slight and despise, and slander. They rape and seduce and silence and ravage. They oppress the powerless. They hurt and torture and maim and murder.

The ultimate power of evil, however, is not found at the level of personal sin. Personal sin is potentiated by its structural realization in sinful systems. Such systems transcend private sin and give evil an urgent power greater than the free disposition of any individual, even though such systems are sustained by the free choices of their participants. Focusing only on the sin of individuals, we may miss the true importance of their personal choices, which is the way they collude in a systemic distortion of reality. The sinful choices of individuals help make spiritual environments of evil, in which genuine humanity is destroyed and God's creation is distorted.

If I physically abuse my wife, then I not only do evil to her by inflicting pain, degrade her human dignity, and break loyalty. I help create an environment in which such abuse is tolerated. I have no capacity to take a stand against such abuse practiced by others. And I participate in an evil pattern that is larger than this one incident.

Sometimes we cannot see the larger pattern until it has grown monstrous. It is startling, for example, to see in contemporary American society such a pattern in the case of children. The evidence clearly supports the hypothesis that, all the rhetoric notwithstanding, contemporary American society is intensely hostile toward children, indeed, that it seeks to become a childless kingdom. All of the romanticization of youth has nothing to do with the love of children and everything to do with wanting to remain children. The evidence is all around us, but few of us have the stomach to see it clearly and see it whole. The millions of abortions, most of them carried out as a means of birth control, are the most tragic example; what violent exercises in rhetorical self-justification must we practice to avoid looking at those stark figures of millions of fetuses killed! Forget for the moment whether they are yet persons. For my argument, I need only note that these fetuses would have become children, and we don't want them. If abortions were all, however, then the pattern would not be so clear. But what follows? Child neglect, physical and sexual abuse, kidnapping, custody battles, child pornography, and child prostitution, and the murderous drug traffic among children. Less obvious is the economic oppression of women and children alike, reflected in the discriminatory costs of food, clothing, shelter, and education. As I understand it, Jesus said, "The way you receive children is the way you receive the kingdom" (Mark 10:15), and we seem to be fairly consistent.

These systems of sinful behavior can grow so large that evil virtually becomes personified. Paul called them the "powers and principalities" (Eph. 3:10) or "the spirit that is now at work in the sons of disobedience" (Eph. 2:2). When Paul discussed the eating of idol meat with the Corinthians, he emphasized that they had freedom to follow their own conscience. If they considered that "idols were not real," then they could freely act on that knowledge and eat meat purchased from a shrine market (1 Cor. 8:4-8). But Paul limited their freedom in two ways. First, individual rights are relativized by the higher responsibility to community identity; each Christian is called on to edify others in the community (8:9-10). If following my conscience means destroying the conscience of another "for whom Christ died" then that is sin, indeed a "sin against Christ" (8:11-13). Second, and even more emphatically, Paul reminds his readers that idols may not be real, but idolatry as a system of meaning and of behavior certainly was real. Participating in idolatrous behavior, Paul suggests, may be participating in the power of demons (10:14-22). The Corinthians therefore ought not to be overconfident (10:12). They need to be aware of the social implications of their behavior.

Christian maturity demands of us, therefore, a complex appreciation of evil in all its dimensions. At the most elementary level, we recognize that our life of faith involves more than a cultivation of the soul or of a small group of friends; it involves a battle "not contending against flesh and blood [other humans] but against the principalities, against the powers, against the world rulers of this present darkness, against the spiritual hosts of wickedness in the heavenly places" (Eph. 6:12), by which Paul means, I think, all the systems of evil and sin in the world. In this battle, we must take sides. And in every disposition of our freedom, we *do* take sides. Yet, the lines of the battle are indistinct when we are in the front lines. It may be easy from a high observation post to detect the movement of troops, but lines are less clear in combat than they appear on maps. For those in the trenches all is smoke and noise and confusion.

In faith, we may choose the gift of God over idolatry. Yet we know that we are implicated in broader systems of idolatry and sin both outside us and within us, shaped by the multiple interactions of our social conditioning and our own past choices. The process of discernment is therefore never ending and never easy; we cannot always detect how the other we encounter presents God's call to us, or when we are to open in embrace or open for combat. Even when we choose unambiguously for good and against evil, we know that we cannot control the consequences of our actions, and that quite without our choosing, our act of faith might feed a larger idolatry. We recognize further our tendency to turn every response of faith into another idolatry, and to close in sin to every new offer of grace from the other. Therefore, precisely in this battle against evil in our own lives and in the world, *we suffer.*

The faithful not only suffer at the hands of sinners who willingly do evil against them. They suffer as well the pain of ambiguity and uncertainty in their own decisions, as well as a sense of despair that comes from measuring the tiny achievements of good against the power of evil let loose in the world. Yet precisely here, the faithful derive their deepest comfort, for amid all the ambiguities of the human battle against evil, there is this one overwhelming certainty: God's battle is also against sin and evil, and in this battle, God associates with suffering.

Jesus and Sin.   This is the deepest significance of the incarnation, that God entered into the human battle on our side against evil. Paul is fond of the language of exchange when describing this alliance, as in his statement that "Christ, though he was rich, yet for your sake became poor, that by his poverty you might become rich" (2 Cor. 8:9). When he wants to state in the most precise terms how "God was in Christ reconciling the world to himself" (2 Cor. 5:19), he uses the exchange most appropriate to the real battle: "For our sake he made him to be sin who knew no sin, so that in him we might become the righteousness of God" (5:21).

The shape of Jesus' ministry as it is described in the Gospels fits this exchange precisely. Jesus did do battle as the stronger one against the powers of evil. He cast out demons and healed the sick, not because healing was his program but because in these physical and spiritual captivities were symbolized the deeper imprisonment of humans in evil. As the servant, "he took our infirmities and bore our diseases," (Isa. 53:4; Matt. 8:17). The diseases he bore were not only those of the body; he took on himself as well the alienation caused by sin. By making himself available to those unclean and unrighteous, Jesus signaled the nature of God's rule as one available to all who will accept it.

In the body language of availability, Jesus challenged the power of sin, which feeds on the symbols and structures of separation and difference, of arrogance and envy, of violent oppression. Jesus' great threat to sin did not come by way of a political revolution against Rome, or by a religious revolt against the Temple cult, but in the simple gesture of treating every person as of equal and infinite worth before God. The challenge was met, as it so often is, by violence. Sin has a stake in the structures of idolatrous power. So Jesus was killed, and in his death "redeemed us from the curse of the law, having become a curse for us—for it is written, 'Cursed be every one who hangs on a tree' " (Gal. 3:13). He experienced every form of alienation and suffering in his battle against sin. But did he fail? Was his death not the victory of sin over righteousness? No, we say, the victory over sin is accomplished by the resurrection (Heb. 9:11-14; 27-28).

But even for those of us who believe that in the resurrection of Jesus, the fundamental victory over evil and sin was accomplished, and that when Jesus "preached to the spirits in prison" (1 Pet. 3:18-19) every realm of human alienation was touched by God's saving power, the visible triumph of good over evil is manifestly not yet accomplished. We are not tempted, as were those early Corinthians, to identify our own personal transformation with the cosmic victory of God over sin and death. Paul had to tell them as a corrective to their enthusiasm: "Then comes the end, when he delivers the kingdom to God the Father after destroying every rule and every authority and power. For he must reign until he has put all his enemies under his feet. The last enemy to be destroyed is death" (1 Cor. 15:24-26). For us, no such corrective is necessary. If anything, the power of evil appears the most obvious of all facts with which we must contend.

Every day we wake to the fresh and appalling evidence: more bodies drugged, more innocents slaughtered, more victims tortured, more minds corrupted. For us it is harder to believe that anything has changed because of Jesus, much less that everything has already been accomplished. We truly walk in hope, in "the conviction of things that are not seen" (Heb. 11:1), and sometimes it is difficult to put one foot in front of another, difficult not to look with despair at our own deep involvement in evil.

At such moments, we do well to remember that we are not the first Christians to have looked with such honesty at the world. Paul was not unacquainted with the fatigue caused by the battle with evil; speaking of "the affliction we experienced in Asia," he says, "We were so utterly, unbearably crushed that we despaired of life itself . . . but that was to make us rely not on ourselves but on God who raises from the dead; he delivered us from so deadly a peril, and he will deliver us; on him we have set our hope, that he will deliver us again" (2 Cor. 1:8-10). And when Paul gazes at the experience of Christians who "suffer at the present time," he declares that "the whole creation has been groaning in travail together until now; and not only the creation, but we ourselves, who have the first fruits of the Spirit, groan inwardly as we wait for adoption as sons, the redemption of our bodies. For this hope we were saved. Now hope that is seen is not hope. For who hopes for what he sees? But if we hope for what we do not see, we wait for it with patience" (Rom. 8:22-25). Patience, we remember, is another word for suffering.

Thinking about Suffering

In the broadest sense, suffering can include everything that we experience, or from the Latin etymology of the term, "undergo" in our lives. Ordinary usage is more specific. First, it denotes receiving rather than doing; it is passive rather than active. Second, it connotes the experience of pain. Thus, we may "suffer" an injury, such as a broken arm, but we take analgesic medicine to relieve the "suffering." A person is dying, and therefore obviously undergoes in passive fashion the ultimate diminishment. Our question, "But is she suffering?" however, addresses itself specifically to the presence of pain. So we say to each other: "I don't mind dying; I just don't want to suffer."

Pain. When we consider suffering as pain, we enter into an extraordinarily complex realm. Pain after all is the only truly subjective category. We are incapable of experiencing another's pain as the other experiences it. We speak of various degrees of pain and tolerances for pain, but even as we speak we must admit that we are only guessing. As outsider, we can estimate pain (and therefore suffering) only by its visible effects. We think that a person screaming non-stop for hours has greater pain and suffering than someone who is silent—silence suggests a control over the pain that the screaming does not. In the absence of other signals, we guess the degree of pain from its effect on function. We think that a headache making a person flinch from bright lights, lie in bed, and vomit is far more severe than one that does not interfere with math computations. An athlete who plays through the pain may be brave, but we instinctively also think she hurts less than the one who sits out the game.

Our only reliable source concerning pain experienced by another is the person who hurts. This means that we are in the realm of personal testimony and of trust. The person who acknowledges personal pain must have some trust in the person to whom it is revealed, that more pain will not thereby be inflicted. A torturer is not told what hurts most. More critically, the person told of pain must trust the revealer, believe what he says, accept his judgment on the degree and kind of pain being experienced. A lack of trust is obviously an enormous problem in contemporary medical attitudes toward and treatment of pain.

The experience of pain is an important test situation for human relationships and values. Since the kind and degree of suffering is not available to observation, we can dismiss the pain of others as trivial, imagined, or exaggerated by invoking some general norm: "That kind of injury *ought not* hurt that badly." We close ourselves to the other's experience because it does not touch us. Or we can go to the other extreme, and become paralyzed by our imagining what someone must be suffering. We forget the protective mechanisms available to a person in pain. We let our imaginations loose, to the point of ourselves participating in the pain. For the one actually in pain, an adjustment may have been made that makes the sufferer accept the pain simply as the way things are. But to the observer the continuance or degree of pain imagined seems intolerable.

We do not find appropriate responses easy to come by, as our delicate and often smudged distinctions between apathy and empathy, sympathy and compassion, indicate. On the side of the sufferer, the experience of pain is also ambiguous. The pain itself may or may not be unmistakable. But the meaning of the pain is often obscure. Did I bring it on myself? Is it a punishment from God? Am I letting down those who rely on me? Am I a failure as a person? Our human habit of measuring worth by accomplishment is particularly noxious when by definition we are not *doing* but *suffering*. One of the most devastating and destructive aspects of pain is the way it demoralizes us and erodes our sense of worth.

Many people, therefore, see suffering above all as a theological or religious test case: the experience of pain challenges the activity and worth of God. How can a loving God permit the suffering of innocent people, especially if that suffering is inflicted by evildoers? How can we reconcile the experience of suffering with a powerful and loving God? If suffering—as so often is the case—is simply defined in terms of evil, then the issue is even sharper. For God to permit suffering is a sign either of powerlessness or of malevolence.

With so much at stake, clear thinking is most necessary; but with so much at stake, clear thinking is almost impossible. Who of us can face unfeelingly the cry of hungry children, the grief of mothers, the depression of the old, the starvation of millions, the desperation of the lonely, the moan of the prisoner, the groan of the dying, the plea of the bewildered, the destruction of cities, the slaughter of birds, the poisoning of fish? Our emotions *are* inevitably engaged; we recoil in fear and loathing before such massive suffering about us.

Our emotions are involved also because each of these things carries a personal story of pain and suffering, from which we cannot absolutely distance ourselves. Our reflections on suffering involve an evaluation of our own lives, with all the possibilities that includes for self-deception and special pleading. Despite the difficulty, we must begin to make distinctions as we think through this dark side of our lives. We need, in particular, to distinguish between the *experiential* aspects of suffering and its *moral* dimensions, even if the applications of those distinctions may need to be revised. To begin this process, I will distinguish kinds of suffering, causes of suffering, and effects of suffering, seeking to locate the religious and moral issues that are raised.

Since suffering is so connected to pain, we can begin by defining pain in a way that applies to every kind of suffering. Pain is a signal that a system in equilibrium is being threatened. Pain is not itself the threat, but the signal of a threat. In this transmission, pain is the link between the system and consciousness. If there is no consciousness, the signal cannot be received or evaluated. If the system has reached the final equilibrium of death, no signal will be sent. Notice that the signal is itself neutral. Notice as well that the question of whether a particular system *ought* to be in a state of equilibrium is an open one.

The Body. The most obvious kind of pain concerns the body. We experience physical pain when injured from without, or when our physical system is threatened by misuse, or when the body is diseased. In these cases, pain is the signal that alerts the body to attend its defenses, our consciousness to begin the process of healing. In contrast to the clear-cut signal function of pain in the case of injury or disease, chronic pain indicates something awry in the signal system itself: damaged nerves, for example, or a systemic disorder deriving from compensation for an earlier trauma. Even in the case of chronic pain, the function of pain is to call attention to the state of the system.

If there is no pain, the body will not respond to threat. We know of children lacking the capacity to feel pain; far from leading joyful lives, they must exercise constant vigilance to avoid self-destruction and are constant prey to injury and disease. Notice as well that when the system is overwhelmed by threat, the body responds with *shock,* a state in which pain is not experienced, but in which the body is far more severely threatened than when it does feel pain. In shock, the body's defensive mechanisms close down to protect the vital processes.

Even in the case of trauma, therefore, physical pain has a positive function. Some pain, furthermore, comes from the threat to physical equilibrium presented by growth. Children experience this pain when they grow very quickly—they are sore all over as they stretch from one body shape to another. Athletes experience it as they develop new muscle capacities. The classic example of such pain is that of childbirth. As sheer physical pain, it is terrifying: the mother's body stretches beyond all reason to allow another body access to the world. But who can call such pain an evil? "When a woman is in travail, she has sorrow, because her hour has come; but when she is delivered of the child, she no longer remembers the anguish, for joy that a child is born into the world" (John 16:21).

Even at the physical level, therefore, pain can have several meanings. By no means is it always negative. Even when the pain experienced is severe and of long duration, the total elimination of pain must mean the elimination of pleasure as well. If we are totally anesthetized, we lose contact with the world as it is, have no chance of encountering the other, and must dwell in the soft limbo of unfeeling.

The Emotions. We also experience pain at the emotional level. Emotions that we experience as painful, such as fear, anxiety, grief, and anger, are equally signals that our emotional system is threatened with disequilibrium. Emotional pain is obviously a complex issue, but it is clear that painful emotions can interact with physical pain in a synergism that heightens and distorts both. The experience of physical pain can create the fear of more pain that can in turn generate a systemic and chronic physical pain, with the cycle spiraling ever more out of control.

Most of us dislike negative feelings in general, and seek to avoid them; when they occur, we hide them or deny them. We want to stay in control. One of the results of our not allowing ourselves to feel or express negative emotions, however, is that the very disequilibrium we fear takes place. And at this level as well, the pain is best understood as a signal. Perhaps our present condition of emotional stability is based on false perceptions or immature closure, and we need to change. Perhaps what we fear as threat is really the call to grow. A neurotic system, after all, is always in some sort of equilibrium; the way to emotional health must pass through disequilibrium and therefore through pain. Indeed, as in the case of the physical state of shock, the emotional state of dysfunction we call *depression* represents a shutting down of emotional responses because of the overwhelming threat of pain; the psyche gathers its wagons in a circle to protect the besieged sense of identity and worth. As in the case of shock, too, depression is all the more serious a condition because of the reduction of pain.

The Mind. We also suffer mental pain. Every time we are required to consider and evaluate new experiences or ideas, our minds must "stretch," which is often a painful process. We must overcome inertia, the comfort of our accustomed perceptions. We experience the new as a threat to our view of the world. The ancient Greeks typically crystallized this truth in a proverb, *mathein pathein*, "to learn is to suffer." None of us would, however, call such pain evil, any more than we do that of childbirthing. A more severe kind of mental pain derives from the massive threat to meaning itself that humans sometimes experience. The term cognitive dissonance is used to describe the clash of ideas and experience that must be resolved one way or another if the person is to continue life in the world. When the threat to meaning is too severe, the mind also may close down and submit to meaninglessness. This is the equivalent of physical shock and emotional depression, and is called *despair*. The mind avoids overall questions of meaning and tends the tiny garden of mental survival. Like shock and depression, despair is all the more dangerous because it no longer experiences sharp pain.

The diverse meanings of human suffering are expressed in its causes as well as its types. Some forms of suffering appear to be necessary corollaries of existence; others are the result of free choice. Much pain accompanies the fact of physical existence. The earth goes through its massive cycles of heat and cold, flood and drought, hurricane and volcanic eruption, bringing to some living things delight and refreshment and to others injury and destruction. Both happen swiftly or slowly, with greater or lesser consciousness, and therefore, with more or less pain. Organisms themselves inevitably pass through stages of generation, growth, decay, and death. The higher the degree of feeling, the more pain accompanies each process. Organisms eat other organisms and are themselves eaten in the great food chain. Human beings must experience the pain of growth and generation if they are to survive; must experience the pain of emotional and mental growth if they are to have culture.

The Necessity of Suffering.   All this suffering is necessary because worldly existence is simply so constituted. If we reject it as evil, then it must be on the basis of a perception other than that of Christian belief, which confesses that the world as it is created is good and reveals the goodness of the God who creates it. We must be like the Buddhists, who see authentic existence as residing in a denial of all physical existence, feeling, and will. Or we must be like the Gnostics who reject the world as the malevolent toy of an evil demiurge. The essential note of Christian realism, however, is the acceptance of such suffering as the corollary of creation. We do not identify physical injury as the willful punishment of a capricious fate; we do not think of illness as a punishment for sin; we do not think of death as the tragic end of a sad existence. Rather, we accept the truth of our existence as creatures. If we are to experience pleasure and joy with others, we must also experience pain and sorrow; if we are to live in God's presence with Jesus, then we must follow the way he has gone and pass through death. We do not rejoice in such suffering, but we rejoice in the gift of creation that has suffering as one of its inevitable components.

Other sorts of pain are not necessary but derive from free human choices. Here we can legitimately raise the question of evil. Yet even here, it is by no means the case that every suffering resulting from freedom *is* evil. Two further distinctions are appropriate: first, between the pain that I inflict on another and the pain I myself embrace; and second, between suffering that is directly inflicted or embraced and that which results indirectly from other choices.

The clearest example of evil is the deliberate infliction of suffering on another creature, simply for the purpose of making the other experience pain. What makes this evil, of course, is not the pain as such but the malevolent intention of the one inflicting the pain and the distortion of truth concerning the "other" involved in that action. We must not do harm to the other who is God's creature and answerable to the Creator alone. We must not manipulate, torture, and damage another intentionally, because to do so means violating them as other, that is, as God's creature and not our possession. Inflicting pain is evil when it distorts the truth of creation.

Sometimes, however, we inflict pain on another as an indirect result of another sort of decision. We may need to do surgery—inflict massive trauma on the body—in order to save a life. We may need to cause emotional pain by disappointing the unrealistic expectations in a child, or by disciplining a child or a student. To meet an idolatrous expectation, or to refrain from necessary discipline, simply because we do not want to cause pain may itself be evil, if it is a distortion of the truth. We may, by protecting another from pain, also prevent them from growing, from becoming the sort of person God wills them to be.

On the other hand, extraordinary caution must be exercised in inflicting pain. Too often humans have justified torture for the sake of God's truth or for the sake of the state; too frequently others have been manipulated, controlled, and made to suffer for their own good. It is the task of discernment to distinguish between that suffering which may result from doing the truth in love, and that which derives from self-righteous sadism.

Corresponding to sadism is the choice of pain for its own sake that we call masochism. At the very least, self-inflicted or invited pain is a distortion of the proper function of pain, which is to act as a signal. Masochism is found at the emotional and spiritual levels as well. The person who takes on the guise of victim, or indulges in a neurotic obsessiveness about guilt, is distorting the truth of the human relationship before God: we must have a project of our own; we cannot live in a state of constant self-abnegation. Furthermore, God is the Judge of our guilt; that is not our business.

At the same time, however, there is a sense in which I can legitimately choose to experience pain as a component in my free choices and as a genuine expression of the obedience of faith. I do this, first, by the acceptance of my creaturely status with all its multiple levels of suffering and by my refusal to reject pain by narcotization or emotional withdrawal. I also "choose pain" when I choose to grow, whether physically (enabling my body to be a strong instrument for service), or emotionally (allowing myself to experience the full range of both joy and sorrow, fear and anger), and mentally (allowing the other to enter my world and redefine my understanding of life).

At a deeper level, the obedience of faith involves suffering and pain in its very structure. When I shape my own project I want it to be absolute. When my project encounters the other, I experience it as a threat to my self-contained universe. When I relativize my project by taking the other into account, I suffer at once the pain of dying (leaving my old-self definition behind) and the pain of growth (stretching into a far broader and more inclusive world). The importance of this sort of suffering cannot be overemphasized for our understanding and practice of Christian spirituality. The very structure of obedience to God involves suffering; avoidance of this suffering means sin, for it is the conscious choice of one's own idolatrous pattern over the gift of God.

The Suffering of Faith.   This is precisely the sort of suffering that the Letter to the Hebrews identifies as essential to the faith of Jesus: "Although he was a Son, he learned obedience through what he suffered; and being made perfect he became the source of eternal salvation to all who obey him" (5:8-9). Hebrews understands Jesus' faith as a progressive opening to God's Word, an opening that was itself suffering. In this painful expansion of his humanity, Jesus progressively *became* "perfect Son," so that what appeared to be the final closure (his death) was in fact a passing through the veil of flesh to share God's life fully (10:19), becoming therefore for us, "pioneer and perfecter" (12:2), pointing the way we are to follow.

Suffering that is part of obedient faith is, in fact, God's carving out a space for his freedom in our hearts. This suffering enlarges our humanity into a greater capacity for God, which implies as well and at the same time a larger capacity for the world as God creates it. This is the perspective of faith, which measures things from a different perspective than that of the world. As Paul says, "I consider that the sufferings of the present time are not worth comparing with the glory [by which he means God's presence] that is to be revealed to us" (Rom. 8:18), and again in 2 Cor. 4:17, "This slight momentary affliction is preparing for us an eternal weight of glory beyond all comparison, because we look not to the things that are seen, but to the things that are unseen for the things that are seen are transient, but the things that are unseen are eternal."

Jesus did not suffer for his own sake alone but for the sake of others. By so doing, he showed us the way in which God "was reconciling the world to himself" by taking on the suffering of humanity and transforming it into an instrument of love. Jesus shows us what it means to "bear one another's burdens" (Gal. 6:2). He was the servant whose obedience to God was spelled out by his love for others: "Christ also suffered for you, leaving you an example, that you should follow in his steps. . . . He himself bore our sins in his body on the tree, that we might die to sin and live to righteousness" (1 Pet. 2:21 and 24).

It is an essential part of the Christian understanding of life that suffering can be taken on for others so that they might have fuller life. Indeed, the highest expression of Christian sanctity is found in this extravagant pouring out of life for the sake of others in generous service. At no point does the classic understanding of Christian existence conflict more directly either with the wisdom of the world or with the wisdom of the gnostic and liberation models of spirituality. Far from being always evil, suffering freely accepted as a service for the life of others can reveal the highest degree of participation in the Spirit of God.

The Eschatological Reservation

The reason why Christians can give some kinds of suffering a positive valuation, and why even negative experiences of suffering can be transformed (never without struggle, to be sure) by the perspective of faith is the same reason why God could reveal love for humans in the suffering Messiah Jesus. The perception of faith is not only that God creates the world at every moment anew, but that God is an infinite source of being and life, and a constant giver of gifts. God calls into being that which is not. God raises the dead to new life.

Jesus endured the suffering of the cross, gave his body as a sacrifice for others, because he did not identify his life with that body or with its survival. Jesus saw his every breath as a gift from God, and knew that if in obedience to God he allowed that gift to be withdrawn, God would restore him to life. Hebrews 12:2 calls Jesus the perfect person of faith, "who for the joy that was set before him endured the cross, despising the shame, and is seated at the right hand of the throne of God." Likewise, Paul described Jesus' refusal to "reckon" equality with God as something to be "possessed," and how Jesus emptied himself out even unto death in obedience, and concluded "Therefore God . . . bestowed on him the name which is above every name" (Phil. 2:9).

It is the hope for a blessed resurrection that distinguishes the Christian perception both of evil and suffering. We do not agree with the view that we only go around once, that this world is really all there is. We cannot supply the content of these convictions. We do not suffer less because of them. We do not deny the reality of pain and evil. But we endure and rejoice because of our conviction that God is Creator, and Judge, and giver of new life. As for proof? We point only to the story of Jesus. We take our stand on that scandalous example and the way it empowers our life here and now with a hope that is already a new, even a resurrection life.

10

Where the Spirit
of the Lord Is,
There Is Freedom

I stated earlier that the path to Christian maturity begins in slavery
and ends in freedom. It is fitting at the end of this book to
consider more directly the goal of Christian growth in the Spirit,
what Paul in Rom. 8:21 calls "the glorious liberty of the children
of God." The reader can expect no more than a sketch of what I
take to be the distinctive Christian understanding of freedom. As
always in this book, I use Paul as the most consistent and reliable
guide for our thinking.

Freedom (or liberty) as the goal of the spiritual life obviously
means something more than free choice, the ability to choose between one thing and another. Freedom denotes rather the most
desirable way of being human in the world. Freedom stands as the
measure of fully authentic humanity. I have argued throughout this
book that freedom is given by faith, the human self-disposition
which accepts life and worth as gift from God. To assess properly
the mature shape of that life of faith, it is helpful to review briefly
what has already been stated about slavery and freedom.

Openness and Closure

I have argued that there is an open-endedness built into human freedom as a corollary of consciousness; in principle, the human spirit can open to the whole world. The openness of the spirit is limited, however, in two important ways: by its location in a body and by its need to become a definite self. The tendency of human freedom is toward premature closure. It wants to become real and definite, and seeks to become so by fixating on some available source of identity. The judgment that closure is "premature" relies on this criterion for authentic human existence: the highest form of humanity is one that shares most in the openness of God towards the world. The point of reference for human identity cannot be any other creature, but only the Creator, who as absolute Spirit transcends all creation and thereby is equally available to all creation.

Every definition of human identity and worth we therefore test on this basis: how much of the world *must* it exclude, and how much of the world *can* it contain? The measure of freedom as the goal of the human spirit is the human person's availability to the world as created by God, or to the world as it truly is in God's sight.

We began our analysis with idolatry, acknowledging at once its inevitability for creatures created without a predetermined center, as well as its absolutizing instinct, the way it makes something partial and contingent into an absolute point of reference for human identity and worth. By making something created an ultimate, idolatry distorts the world: it renders grotesque the thing made absolute, and it closes off other relative but no less real dimensions of the world. The closure that is idolatry can occur at several levels. The first and most obvious is the level of bodily existence, whether the point of reference is the body itself (its survival, health, pleasure, beauty) or its extension in possessions. A fixation with the physical distorts the body by making it too important, and restricts the freedom of the human spirit to a very narrow scope. Fixation at the level of emotional equanimity or mental comfort, we saw, involves the same truncation of the spirit.

I have defined grace as God's gift of otherness, made available in creation at every moment. This gift calls us out of our narrow projects of self-definition. I have defined sin as the conscious refusal of the other for the sake of one's idolatrous project. Sin is distinguished from idolatry by being a slavery freely and consciously chosen. In idolatry we place ourselves as servants to something which we treat as ultimate; sin potentiates the error by obedience to a project that we *know* is not ultimate but insist on treating as ultimate.

Paul's statement in Rom. 14:23 has provided us with our basic framework in this discussion: "whatever does not proceed from faith is sin." Paul delineates the two responses available to humans who have been presented with the gift of God. If sin is the refusal of otherness and a consequent closure of the self, faith is the acceptance of the gift from the Other with an accompanying openness of the self. Faith is defined by an openness to the One who is totally Other but who gifts us in the specific and concrete others we encounter every day. Faith does not close on any single aspect of the world, but defines the self in relationship to the One who transcends all the world and by transcending is related equally to all that exists. Faith's freedom resides in the simple fact that by being related to the One who is open to all things, we thereby are enabled to be open to all things.

The issue is not whether human freedom must center itself, but on the adequacy of that in which it centers. Paul works wonderful changes on the terms *slavery, obedience,* and *freedom* in this key passage: "Do you not know that if you yield yourselves to any one as obedient slaves, you are slaves of the one whom you obey, either of sin, which leads to death, or obedience [note that Paul here as throughout Romans means faith] which leads to righteousness" (Rom. 6:16)? For Paul, humans are inevitably slaves of something, that is, centered in something they treat as ultimate and obey in the ordering of their lives. He sees the two options as sin and faith. One leads to death. The other leads to righteousness. He continues, "Thanks be to God, that you who were once slaves of sin have become obedient from the heart to the standard of teaching to which you were committed, and, having been set free from sin, have become slaves of righteousness. I am speaking in human terms, because of your natural limitations. For just as you once yielded your members to impurity and to greater and greater iniquity, so now yield your members to righteousness for sanctification" (6:17-19). In this last part of Paul's statement, he points us to the fact that each orientation (sin or faith) has a pattern of life appropriate to it; having chosen faith, Christians are to live out the pattern of righteousness that leads to sanctification—what we have been calling Christian maturity.

The openness that is an essential dimension of faith must, of course, be carefully qualified. The freedom of faith is constrained by the limitations of body, emotion, mind, and society that form the context of our human lives. And we have seen as well that the response of faith can never be once-for-all. Every response of obedience to God's gift, in fact, tends to become another plateau on which we want to rest, another (if higher) form of idolatry to which we want to cling. The life of faith is a constant oscillation between the poles of idolatry and obedience. The freedom of faith, in other words, is never a product completely accomplished before death but a process that continues until death.

Because they miss this complex character of faith, both the gnostic and liberation models of spirituality turn freedom into a program of human endeavor rather than a process of response to the Other, whose gift is the necessary condition to breaking the patterns of idolatry.

In one sense, the gnostic model is all about freedom. The authentic self is locked in materiality as a prisoner of darkness. The soul will not be truly free until the flesh is shed and the spirit returns to the light from which it came. The freedom of the soul is accomplished by the mortification of the flesh and the control of emotional impulses. Paradoxically, this requires constant care and vigilance. Total self-control demands a compulsive preoccupation with the self and defense against the powers that threaten the self. The gnostic model does not make entirely clear either what this internal freedom of the spirit is *for*. Certainly it has nothing to do with other people or the structures of society. All that counts is the liberation of the self, for the self is all that is truly real or worthwhile.

The gnostic is a prisoner of ideology, caught by its presuppositions in narrow perceptions of the world and the human condition. The gnostic spirituality is doomed to rigidity and inflexibility. The gnostic *cannot* celebrate the body, other persons, or the world, because they are all by definition implicated in evil. The system can only give one answer to each question. Eat or don't eat? Don't eat, for the body must die. Sex or no sex? None, for the body is evil. Commit myself to the care of others? No, for I am a pilgrim passing through an evil place and must travel alone and light. There is no ambiguity, but there is also no choice. The system decides every choice beforehand. No new data is allowed in, no other possibilities can be entertained. Faith is reduced to a program; and in the process, freedom disappears.

The liberation model also is all about freedom, as the name itself suggests. It sees people as captive to evil social structures. People will be truly themselves only when they are removed from oppression, from capitalistic economic systems, from hunger, or from sexism and racism and ageism and specieism. Destructive social systems must themselves be destroyed and replaced by others more humane. Then, it is supposed, the natural goodness of people can express itself spontaneously. As in the gnostic model, the ideal of freedom from is much clearer than the goal of freedom for. And once again, the pathway to structural freedom demands the exercise of control, this time through social engineering. Experience suggests that people tend to act in the same old selfish ways even within egalitarian structures. If society is going to remain equal, there is the need for continuing vigilance and control, which means, at the societal level, the need for continuing coercive mechanisms. The liberation of the social order seems to require as paradoxical corollary its participants' captivity.

The liberationist too is caught in the iron grip of ideological consistency, which demands in practice a remarkable rigidity and inflexibility. Only one kind of social system can be good. We cannot even imagine a humane capitalism, for our ideology has defined capitalism as evil. We cannot consider any male leadership as benign, for patriarchalism is evil in any mode. Activity which does not directly advance the cause of the movement must be considered as counter-revolutionary. Social engineers whose reforms are based on an ideology also find themselves in the embarrassing position of having only one answer for every question. They are like structural engineers who can build only one size bridge no matter how wide the river, or like carpenters who can build only one style house no matter what the climate. Faith is reduced to a program, and in the process, freedom disappears.

Freedom from What and for Whom

Paul characteristically rejects the reduction of faith to a simple flight from the world or flight to the world, and insists that faith requires living out a tension within which we make choices for God in the complex and ambiguous contexts of the world. When we turn to Paul's understanding of Christian freedom, we find the same tension. After completing his long argument against the idolatrous claims of the circumcizers, Paul tells the Galatians, "For freedom Christ has set us free. . . Do not submit again to a yoke of slavery" (Gal. 5:1). But shortly thereafter in Gal. 5:13, Paul adds, "You were called to freedom brethren; only do not use your freedom as an opportunity for the flesh, but through love be servants of one another. For the whole law is fulfilled in one word, 'you shall love your neighbor as yourself.'" Christian freedom therefore exists in a tension between the freedom from which has already been accomplished, and the freedom for which points the direction of growth into full maturity.

The most distinctive note in this Pauline understanding of freedom is that it is not a future goal to be accomplished by human effort, but a reality brought about already by God's *gift*. Left to ourselves we remain inevitably idolators, locked in the circle of compulsion. But faith tells us that we have not been left alone. We have been gifted by otherness. And it is the offer from the Other that breaks the circle of compulsion and enables us to be free. Thus, Paul says that we have been freed from fear, the flesh, sin, death, and the law.

We have been freed from fear, for the love of God has been poured into our hearts by the Holy Spirit (Rom. 5:5), giving us the boldness of free access to the source of our being and worth, the Creator (5:1). We have no need to be terrified either by isolation or emptiness, for we are not alone and we are filled. God has first accepted us, so that we can call God, "Abba, Father!" (8:15). We are also freed from the flesh. By the flesh Paul means every form of idolatrous impulse, especially that manifested in antisocial behavior. Because the gift of the Spirit establishes our being and worth before God, we no longer need to create our own worth through our power and possessions; we do not need to engage in fratricidal competition to be "best son," for we have been equally gifted as "children of God" (8:14).

We are freed from sin, for sin is precisely the hardened project formed by the engines of fear and compulsion to which we cling so tightly that we close ourselves to any definition from another, close ourselves indeed to the gift of otherness that is God's grace. Thus, Paul says that even while we were still sinners, were enemies of God, God reached across the barrier of our isolation with the knowledge and love that frees us (Rom. 5:6-11).

We are freed even from death, for it is the fear of death and nothingness, the fear of our contingent condition, that drives us to shape idols out of our compulsion (Heb. 2:14-15). But now we know that God's love comes to us from one who has passed through death to new life in the presence and power of God, and has given us a share in that life by the gift of the Spirit: "Where the Spirit of the Lord is, there is freedom (2 Cor. 3:17).

We are freed finally from the law, for even the "holy and just and good" commandment of God (Rom. 7:12) could be manipulated by us as a means of self-aggrandizement, so that our very virtue could be used as a bribe to win a favorable judgment from God (7:7-12). Given God's gift of the Spirit, we are free to accept God's gift of righteousness not on our own terms, but on God's, through the faith of the Messiah (3:21-26). Empowered by that Spirit, we can finally "fulfill the just requirement of the law" (8:4).

Because of the gift of love given through the Holy Spirit, we have "the freedom of the children of God" (Rom. 8:21). This means that we do not need to grasp at any portion of the world to make it the source of our being and worth. The world as such has indeed been given to us with all else: "Let no one boast of men. For all things are yours, whether Paul or Apol'los or Cephas or the world or life or death or the present or the future, all these are yours; and you are Christ's; and Christ is God's" (1 Cor. 3:21-22). Neither are we required to flee any part of the world as a threat to our freedom: "Who will separate us from the love of Christ? Shall tribulation, or distress, or persecution, or famine, or nakedness, or peril, or sword? . . . In all these things we are more than conquerors through him who loved us. For I am sure that neither death, nor life, nor angels, nor principalities, nor things present, nor things to come, nor powers, nor height nor depth, nor anything else in all creation, will be able to separate us from the love of God in Christ Jesus our Lord" (Rom. 8:35-39). Christian freedom therefore is based in the gift of *God's* love toward us.

What, then, does Paul see freedom *for*? His most powerful statement appears to be a tautology: "for freedom Christ has set us free" (Gal. 5:1). A closer reading, however, shows that Paul has something definite in mind. Freedom must first *remain* freedom; it cannot turn back to any form of enslavement. Having received the gift of love, and with it our being and identity and worth, we cannot return to a way of life predicated on the lack of that gift. So Paul says that we are not to live according to the flesh, that is, engage in self-serving competition against the neighbor (Gal. 5:13-15). But neither are we to live according to Torah, that is, define our relationship to God and world in a way that bypasses the gift of love in the

Messiah and its restructuring of those relationships; Torah cannot be the ultimate norm of our righteousness or of the demands of love (5:1).

Positively, the freedom given us by the gift of God's love in the Holy Spirit *empowers us*, so that we can share that *same* gift with others. God became open to us and available to us in the gift of the Messiah Jesus. So are we to open ourselves to the world, make ourselves available to each other. But just as the call of God comes to us in new circumstances every day and can never safely be predicted, so do the needs of our neighbor change moment by moment. Openness to those needs is what freedom is for. Empowered by the Spirit, freed from the need to be closed and self-protective because of the absolute affirmation given by God's gift of love, we can finally answer yes to the other as other, the neighbor whom we encounter every day.

Christian freedom is *for* others. "Bear one another's burdens, and so fulfill the law of Christ [the norm of the Messiah] (Gal. 6:2). The freedom that is ours by gift from the Spirit of God *enables* us to dispose of our selves without losing our selves. The Holy Spirit empowers our spirit to be available to the world in service. This service, furthermore, is defined not by our preoccupation or blueprint for perfection but by the real and specific needs of others. Among them, God's project is being shaped at every moment, and it calls us to obedient faith, self-donating love.

The Gift of Simplicity

Deep within the human heart is the longing for simplicity and for the peace that is its silent accompanist. For some, the longing for simplicity is a sort of nostalgia for lost innocence, a return to a world in which complexity and the tension it generates do not exist. But such simplicity is really worthless; naivete is not Christian maturity, because it does not deal with the world as it truly is. The real world is complex and filled with tensions.

The gnostic and liberation models of spiritualities offer a kind of simplicity, but it is accomplished by the elimination of complexity and tension through ideology and program. The simplicity that is given by compulsion is artificial and rigid; it can endure only by constant attention to its own protection, and the elimination of any other that threatens it.

The traditional Shaker song has it right, I think: "It's a gift to be simple, it's a gift to be free." We have seen how for Christians, to be free comes by way of gift. I suggest that true simplicity is derived as well from the same gift of God's love that makes us free.

Such simplicity is neither naivete nor closed compulsiveness. It is rather the transparency that comes from willing one thing. The one thing willed, however, is not a thing among other things, but the Source of all things. Faith is centered in the One who transcends all things and is thereby available to all things, and since faith is centered in what does not appear it is also thereby available to all that does appear.

The freedom of Christian maturity is the freedom of accessibility. The freedom of the saint is precisely characterized by simple and unaffected presence to the world. Because the saint is not preoccupied with defending the self or its possessions, she is able to see the other as other. Indeed, the other is received not as threat but as gift. Because the saint does not seek identity or worth from any created thing, she uses things properly in their created order. She perceives persons as ends in themselves, not as means to the saint's projects.

The saint is open to what is new and different, because he expects from the new a gift from God, and from the different an opportunity to grow into a world as expansive as God's. Because the saint's righteousness is defined not in terms of doing this thing or that thing, but rather by the obedience of faith in God, he is free to do either this thing or that with a directness and simplicity that are totally lacking in second guessing or neurotic anxiety. Because the saint trusts in God, trust in others is available.

The saint progressively realizes the command of Paul, "If we live by the Spirit, let us also walk by the Spirit" (Gal. 5:25). This freedom in the Spirit is not an achievement that must be guarded or a program that must be imposed, but a deep openness to new circumstances and invitations. The saint can be led by the Spirit in creative responses to the needs of other bodies and persons in the world. This freedom does not have only one answer to every question; it truly hears each question and so hears also the answer contained in it. It does not demand an absolute consistency of itself, of others, or of God, but adapts itself joyously—if not without suffering—to God's new projects.

The Freedom of Jesus

We have repeatedly turned to Paul's affirmation that we have received the Spirit of adoption, so that we can address God as Jesus did, "Abba, Father" (Gal. 4:6). In the place where that exultant exclamation occurs, Paul carefully develops a contrast between the condition of a child, which he calls "no better than a slave," to the condition of sons who have entered into their maturity at "the date set by the father" (Gal. 4:2). His entire point about the reception of the Spirit is that it is to replicate in our freedom the messianic pattern of the Son whom "God sent forth . . . born of a woman, born under the law, to [redeem] [liberate] those who were under the law, so that we might receive adoption as sons" (4:4-5). So are we to move in freedom from childhood to maturity: we are meant by God to have free access to the estate's property; to be available to the world within our embodied condition, as God is in the unconditionedness of absolute Spirit; to have the world as accessible to us in the part in which we dwell as it is in its entirety to the God who creates it: "So through God you are no longer a slave but a son, and if a son then an heir" (4:7).

We are correct, then, to look this last time at Jesus, the pioneer and perfecter of faith (Heb. 12:3), in order to understand what it means to have "the glorious liberty of the children of God" (Rom. 8:21). In all the times I have read the Gospels over the years, this is one truth whose light has never dimmed for me, whose impact has never lost its power: Jesus appears in the Gospels as a truly free human being. Do the Gospels accurately represent him as he actually existed? Or do they describe Jesus according to the perceptions of faith? It does not matter, for in either case, we find in Jesus' simplicity and freedom the author of our own identity, and the measure of Christian maturity.

Jesus' freedom was defined by faithful obedience to God and service to others. We see in him first freedom from. Even his enemies attested that he knew no fear of other humans (Mark 12:14). He was therefore able to say with perfect clarity, "Do not fear those who kill the body but cannot kill the soul. Rather fear him who can destroy both soul and body in hell" (Matt. 10:28). Because Jesus feared God alone, he was not afraid of conflict with evil; he could enter the tombs, filled as they were with the violence of demonic derangement, cast out the evil spirit, and restore a person to health (Mark 5:1-20). He did not fear the power of the authorities, but could speak bold prophecy to them: "Go tell that fox, 'Behold, I cast out demons and perform cures today and tomorrow, and the third day I finish my course' " (Luke 13:32). He did not fear pollution by food or by people. He could reach out and touch the leper to restore him to human society (Mark 1:40). He could eat at the tables of the outcast (Mark 1:15-17) as well as at the banquets of the powerful (Luke 14:1).

Because Jesus was free of fear, he was also free from compulsion. There was nothing he possessed that he needed to protect with all his energy and attention; therefore he could be attentive to the world around him. Since he was not defined by a perfectionism of escape from the world, he could associate with anyone, both the righteous and the unrighteous (Mark 2:16-17). He could eat anywhere (Mark 7:1-2), sleep anywhere (4:38), and talk with any person (John 4:7-26). Because Jesus was open to the world, he was the most accessible of all persons. Outcasts of every sort were drawn to him (Mark 1:40; Luke 15:1), sought his touch (Mark 5:27-28). And Jesus reached out and touched them. Little children found a home in the arms of Jesus (Mark 10:16).

Jesus was free from compulsion in another sense. He did not define his messianic mission in terms of a specific program in which ideological purity required translation into social structure. He did not identify the rule of God with Jewish control of the land, so that for God to rule the hated Roman oppressors needed to be driven out. He did not identify the kingdom of God with the perfect observance of Torah, so that for God to rule the ordinary people needed to be excluded. He did not identify the kingdom of God with a ritual purity, so that for God to rule all the elect needed to live apart from the world.

Because he did not identify God's rule with such programs, Jesus allowed God to rule his heart in faithful obedience. This freed him to be available to respond to God's project in the cares and concerns, the needs and projects of those he encountered every day. Jesus did not need to protect his time and energy, his ideas and presence for bigger and better things. He was the servant who revealed that there is no project bigger or better than the presence of God to the world, and who demonstrated that presence in the time and space, the energy and ideas and compassion he shared with all the little ones of the earth (see Matt. 8:17; 12:18-21).

Because Jesus did not seek to establish himself by his own purity or program but lived by every word that came from the mouth of

God (Matt. 4:4), did not seek to secure his life as a possession but received it moment by moment as a gift from the Father (Matt. 11:25), did not stand on his own righteousness but to the very end committed his spirit to the Father from whom he had received it (Luke 23:46), Jesus reveals himself as the "Yes" of humans to God as well as the "Yes" of God to us (2 Cor. 1:20), the head from which all the body of humanity draws its growth and maturity (Col. 2:19), the glory of God in a human person, fully alive with the freedom of the spirit, simple as God is simple in an open embrace of all the world.

Epilogue

I was asked by the editors to provide my readers with some notion of the sources that have contributed to this book. This seemed like a simple request but it turned out to be impossible to fulfill. As I mentioned in the preface, I am indebted to many writers far superior to me. But since I began serious reading in these matters some thirty-odd years ago, it becomes increasingly difficult to sort out the credits.

Readers already knowledgeable in various areas will certainly spot the obvious dependencies: my broadly Aristotelian/Thomistic philosophical framework, for example, well-laced with the existentialism of thinkers like Søren Kierkegaard, Martin Buber, Jose Ortega y Gasset, and Gabriel Marcel. My main theological influence is obviously Karl Rahner, with significant leavening by Hans Urs von Balthasar, Henri de Lubac, Edward Schillebeeckx, and others. Peter Berger's way of viewing society is patently operative. So is the language about religious experience associated with Rudolf Otto and Mircea Eliade. But the influence of Bronislaw Malinowski, and Clifford Geertz, Erich Fromm, Norman Cohn, and Rosabeth Kantor (on the first topic) and of Gerardus Van der Leeuw, Joachim Wach, and I. M. Lewis (on the second topic) is no less real. My fondness for speaking of the human "project" is owed to Adrian Van Kaam, although he might not recognize my way of employing it. The same can be said for my language about mystery and hope: Gabriel Marcel and William Lynch both affect that but so do Rahner and Odo Casel.

And so on for every topic treated: Odo Casel and Louis Bouyer deeply influenced my views of liturgy, but so did Johannes Huizinga, Josef Pieper, Jean Daniélou, Josef Jungmann, and Adrian Kavanagh. As for the overall approach to spirituality, I am always aware of the importance Thomas Merton had on me as for my whole generation. But no less am I indebted to figures such as Dom Columba Marmion, Bernard Basset, Hubert Van Zeller, John Knox, and Robert Capon and all the armies of spiritual writers back to Origen on prayer and martyrdom. Most of all, I am always conscious and grateful for the healthy vision of the world I received from the greatest of my personal intellectual heros, G. K. Chesterton.

The point I am trying to make concerns not the extent of my reading but its thoroughly variegated character. This book, for better or worse, represents a very personal vision of the life of the Spirit, distilled in part from all these years of reading, but even more from years of living and observing others live, of listening to others and thinking about what I have heard.

It may be more useful to any reader who likes what is contained here to know how this small book fits into the larger theological project I have been working on. The project is motivated by the conviction that the proper task of theology is the discernment of God's work in the world, but that Christians are inhibited in their ability to think theologically because the three essential components for such a process of discernment are deficient: the ability to perceive Scripture as transparent to human religious experience; the ability to perceive our own human experience flexibly and faithfully with the symbols of Scripture; a community of discernment within which the disparate experiences of individuals are elevated to a narrative of faith.

The books I have written for Fortress Press are all parts of an attempt to think creatively about theology as a process within the church, by addressing these deficiencies. In *Writings of the New Testament: An Interpretation* (1986), I try to read all of the New Testament writings as a literature generated by religious experience and reshaping the symbols of Torah. In the epilogue to that book, I propose a canonical model for the continuing reading of the New Testament in the church. A second element of the process is dealt with in the book *Decision Making in the Church: A Biblical Model* (1983). There I speak of decision making as a hermeneutical process, an articulation of faith by which communities try to discern the narrative of God's action in their midst by attentive listening to human experience and by rereading the symbols of Scripture in the light of what God is doing. Even earlier, I wrote a book called *Sharing Possessions: Mandate and Symbol of Faith* (1981). Some of the themes of the present book are anticipated in that earlier study whose specific focus was one aspect of Christian existence, the mystery of being and having. I tried to show that a careful exegesis of all the Scriptures must be informed as well by a careful exegesis of human experience, language, and social forms, if we are to talk seriously about the use of the Bible for life.

The present book fits into this overall project by providing my reading of human existence as one gifted constantly by God but also driven by patterns of fear and compulsion, and therefore best described as an oscillation between idolatry and faith. I hope to have provided some sense of how individual and community lives might be "read" flexibly and creatively as dramas of idolatry, sin, grace, and faith. If I have been at all successful, perhaps I have given some clues to those caught between modernity and tradition as to how they can begin to "read" their own lives in terms of an intelligent faith. If so, then the texts of Scripture should in turn take on new life, and the need for a community of such living discernment and discourse appear even more urgent.